BEST OF

Turin

Sally O'Brien

Best of Turin
1st edition – July 2005

Published by Lonely Planet Publications Pty Ltd
ABN 36 005 607 983

Australia	Head Office, Locked Bag 1, Footscray, Vic 3011
	☎ 03 8379 8000 fax 03 8379 8111
	🖳 talk2us@lonelyplanet.com.au
USA	150 Linden St, Oakland, CA 94607
	☎ 510 893 8555 toll free 800 275 8555
	fax 510 893 8572
	🖳 info@lonelyplanet.com
UK	72–82 Rosebery Avenue, London EC1R 4RW
	☎ 020 7841 9000 fax 020 7841 9001
	🖳 go@lonelyplanet.co.uk

This title was commissioned in Lonely Planet's London office and produced by: **Commissioning Editor** Michala Green **Coordinating Editor** Craig Kilburn **Assisting Editor** Monique Choy **Coordinating Cartographer** Daniel Fennessy **Layout Designer** Laura Jane **Cartographers** Anthony Phelan, Jenny Jones **Managing Cartographer** Mark Griffiths **Cover Designer** Annika Roojun **Cover Artwork** Brendan Dempsey **Project Manager** Eoin Dunlevy **Mapping Development** Paul Piaia **Thanks to** Elena Cottini and Daniela Vitta at Studio Mailander, and Città di Torino, for help and support

© Lonely Planet Publications Pty Ltd 2005.

Photographs by Martin Lladó/Lonely Planet Images except for the following: p14, p16, p21 and p26 Sally O'Brien, p23 and p32 Neil Setchfield/Lonely Planet Images, p48 and p87 Alan Benson/Lonely Planet Images, p49 Martin Moos/Lonely Planet Images, p82 Jon Davison/Lonely Planet Images. All images are copyright of the photographers unless otherwise indicated. **Cover photograph** Mole Antonelliana, Enzo Signorelli/Alamy Images. All images are copyright of the photographers unless otherwise indicated. Many of the images in this guide are available for licensing from Lonely Planet Images: 🖳 www.lonelyplanetimages.com

ISBN 1 74104 283 6

Printed by Markono Print Media Pte Ltd
Printed in Singapore

Acknowledgments Turin Metro Map © 2004 Gruppo Turinese Trasporti

HOW TO USE THIS BOOK

Colour-Coding & Maps

Each chapter has a colour code along the banner at the top of the page which is also used for text and symbols on maps (eg all venues reviewed in the Highlights chapter are orange on the maps). The fold-out maps inside the front and back covers are numbered from 1 to 6. All sights and venues in the text have map references; eg, (4, B5) means Map 4, grid reference B5. See p128 for map symbols.

Prices

Multiple prices listed with reviews (eg €10/5) usually indicate adult/concession admission to a venue. Concession prices can include senior, student, member or coupon discounts. Meal cost and room rate categories are listed at the start of the Eating and Sleeping chapters, respectively.

Text Symbols

☎	telephone
✉	address
🖳	email/website address
€	admission
☉	opening hours
ⓘ	information
🚌	bus
🚆	train
🚋	tram
P	parking available
♿	wheelchair access
✕	on site/nearby eatery
👶	child-friendly venue
V	good vegetarian selection

Contents

From the Publisher

AUTHOR

Sally O'Brien

A frequent visitor to Italy, Sally leapt at the chance to spend some time in Turin and whittle her experiences there down to a pocket-sized format – no mean feat in a city filled with charms. Sadly, it seems that her reputation for creative driving preceded her and she was denied the chance to stuff the gearbox of a FIAT ('Fix It Again Tony!') on the roof at Lingotto.

Thanks to Michala, Duncan, Claudia, Francesca, Paola, Barbara, Giorgia, Pierfranco, Cristina, Ugo, Ernesto, Emanuela, Roberta, Tiziana, Luisella, Alessandro, Laura, Eric, Federico, Graham and Simon for showing me so many good times in Turin. Thanks to Craig Kilburn, Daniel Fennessy and Laura Jane at Lonely Planet Melbourne. A big thanks to Ric Birch for his generosity and help with the Winter Olympics special section, and *mille grazie* to Elena Cottini and Damir Biuklic, Turin's wittiest hypochondriac and man about town *par excellence*.

PHOTOGRAPHER

Martin Lladó

Martin Lladó, a freelance photographer and writer, lives in Copenhagen with his wife Minna and their son Simon. Martin has worked with Lonely Planet since 1998 and has until now visited some 35 different countries.

Martin enjoyed an intense and varied 10-day photo shoot in Piedmont's capital. Turin was sunny and warm. Turin was rainy and chilly. Turin was tasty. Turin was fun. Turin was challenging. But mostly it was sheer pleasure and a privilege to portray this cultural and sporty city on the rise.

Martin sends his thanks to all the good people at Studio Mailander for their help and enjoyable company, especially Barbara Papuzzi and Elena Cottini. Thanks a bunch also goes out to Angelo Pittro of EDT - Lonely Planet's Italian publishing partner based in the heart of Turin.

SEND US YOUR FEEDBACK

We love to hear from travellers – your comments keep us on our toes and help make our books better. Our well-travelled team reads every word on what you loved or loathed about this book. Although we cannot reply individually to postal submissions, we always guarantee that your feedback goes straight to the appropriate authors, in time for the next edition – and the most useful submissions are rewarded with a free book. To send us your updates – and find out about Lonely Planet events, newsletters and travel news – visit our award-winning website: 💻 **www.lonelyplanet.com/feedback.**

Note: We may edit, reproduce and incorporate your comments in Lonely Planet products such as guidebooks, websites and digital products, so let us know if you don't want your comments reproduced or your name acknowledged. For a copy of our privacy policy visit 💻 www.lonelyplanet.com/privacy.

Introducing Turin

And you thought the Renaissance took place in another time and place! Turin, unfairly burdened with a reputation for little more than industry, a football team and a shroud, has emerged from its cocoon and taken flight as Italy's butterfly.

The city has embarked with gusto on one of the largest urban rejuvenation programmes ever, with reclaimed land enriched by innovative redevelopment, factories turned into cultural spaces, infrastructure improved to accommodate locals and visitors, a stunningly perfect position that sees both the mountains and the sea within easy reach and a love of art that literally lights up the city streets at night.

Turin works hard but gives the impression that enjoyment is every bit as important to its inhabitants, with gastronomy and cocktail hour uppermost in everyone's mind. Her streets are lined with porticoes and baroque or Art-Nouveau confections and her *piazze* are filled with greenery and cafés. A love of tradition doesn't stop the city from moving forward and looking to the future. The city feels like a modern-day pleasuredome that's still a well-kept secret – but with the 2006 Winter Olympics, you can be sure that this place is about to hit the front page, and for all the right reasons. Spread the word – Turin really is magic.

Palazzo Reale

Neighbourhoods

Turin's chessboard-like design system aids travellers. In this guide, we have divided the city as follows. **Il Centro** is where many historic buildings lie. It is south of Via Po, east of Corso Re Umberto I, north of Corso Vittorio Emanuele II, has a diagonal border with Via Pietro Micca and extends to Piazza Castello. It includes Via Roma and is bordered to the east by the Po. The **Quadrilatero Romano** extends west of Piazza Castello to Corso Principe Eugenio and Corso Inghilterra, with its southern borders at Via Pietro Micca and Via Cernaia. The area known as Borgo Dora is also included in this. This area also holds pedestrianised Via Giuseppe Garibaldi, Piazza Statuto and Stazione Porta Susa, which is set to become the city's main train station. **Piazza Castello to the Po** includes the streets east of Via XX Settembre, down to Via Giuseppe Garibaldi and north of Via Po, with its eastern border at the River Po. Piazza Vittorio Veneto is included in this definition, and Mole Antonelliana is its most obvious landmark. **La Cittadella** encompasses the streets south of Via Cernaia and west and southwest of Corso Re Umberto I, plus the residential areas known as La Crocetta and San Paolo and the streets immediately to the west of Stazione Porta Nuova. **San Salvario & Around** means east of Via Nizza and south of Corso Vittorio Emanuele II, while **Lingotto** means exactly that – the streets that surround the massive former FIAT factory and the building itself. **Over the Po** is the area often referred to as La Collina or Borgo Po that lies east of the river.

In terms of character, Il Centro is the area that people tend to work, shop, dine and lounge in, with its numerous piazze, baroque palaces, historic cafés and shops filled with fashion and antiques. Quadrilatero Romano is a former working-class district with lots of history that has been rediscovered, with wine bars, restaurants and funky and/or artisanal shops plying their wares to in-the-know locals. Piazza Castello to the Po holds a number of sights, plus businesses catering to the university and the university itself. La Cittadella is generally a residential area, with some very good Liberty and Art-Nouveau buildings and a general aura of subdued good taste. Lingotto contains few sights as such, but is getting a thorough makeover for the Winter Olympics, while Over the Po is wealthy, green and residential.

Off the Beaten Track

Generally, the only time you'll feel hemmed in by crowds in Turin is if you venture out for a stroll along Via Roma, Via Po or Via Garibaldi, especially on weekend afternoons. If you simply must find solitude, head to Parco del Valentino on weekdays, Parco Naturale di Superga anytime, Parco della Mandria, Basilica di Superga when the tombs aren't open, or some of the city's lesser-known museums, palaces and galleries, which all tend to be quiet from Tuesday to Friday (and closed on Monday). If you're seeking a quiet meal, going to lunch before 1pm or dinner before 8.30pm will generally guarantee some p&q.

Itineraries

Turin, like most Italian cities, serves up beauty, history and enjoyment on a platter, and it's possible to explore the Roman, medieval, baroque, industrial and Art-Nouveau past on Turin's chessboard, with ruins, churches, palaces, museums, galleries, courtyards, *piazze,* restaurants, cafés and bars all tempting you to step inside and delve deeper into the city. Turin is easily navigated, and public transport is not only good – it's getting better (see p113).

DAY ONE

First things first – *bicerin* (a hot chocolate coffee and cream delight) from Al Bicerin (p84) at Piazza della Consolata. Head across the piazza to Chiesa della Consolata (Santuario di Maria Consolatrice, or La Consolata, p39), then stroll down bustling Via Garibaldi, a pedestrianised mall, to Piazza Castello (p37) before a visit to Mole Antonelliana (p8) and a stirring view over the city. Take lunch at La Vitel Etonné (p69) before visiting the Basilica di Superga (p15) for more wonderful views and a visit to the tombs. Back in the centre of town, cocktail hour beckons at Tre Galli (p90) or L'Obelix (p90), before dinner at AB+ (p72).

Lowlights
- Dog poo everywhere
- River Po mosquitoes in summer
- Finding a place to park
- Trying to understand the public transport map
- Most attractions being closed on Mondays

DAY TWO

Visit lively Porta Palazzo markets (p12) in the morning and then explore Museo Egizio (p13) or Galleria Sabauda (p18) until lunchtime, when you take your place at La Pista (p81) in Lingotto before entering the Pinacoteca Giovanni e Marella Agnelli (p16). A stroll through the Parco del Valentino (p40) or along the River Po will show you how verdant Turin really is, and give you an appetite for yet another Piedmontese feast.

DAY THREE

Head to Castello di Rivoli (p10) and lunch at Combal.Zero (p72) then make your way to either Palazzina di Caccia di Stupinigi (p21) or Fondazione Sandretto Re Rebaudengo (p14) depending on your appetite for old or new. After dinner, prepare to kick on with a night on the tiles at the clubs of Murazzi or in Docks Dora (p92).

Take a peek in the 'jewellery box' gallery

Highlights

MOLE ANTONELLIANA (4, H4)

Turin's most memorable and remarkable sight is the Mole Antonelliana, which towers over the city a few blocks from Via Po. When construction commenced in 1863 it was intended to be a synagogue and rapidly assumed white-elephant status within 10 years. This extraordinary structure, which stands at 167m, is truly captivating and awe-inspiring when spied from the surrounding narrow streets of the neighbourhood. Capped by an aluminium spire, it is engineering as an art form (in a similar vein perhaps to the Eiffel Tower) and a delicious architectural folly combined. When illuminated at night, it's a spectral sight, and when the Luci d'Artista exhibition is on (November to January), you can find Mario Merz's contribution creeping up the dome in the guise of the Fibonacci series (it's a maths thing…).

INFORMATION

☎ 011 812 56 58

▢ www.museonazion aledelcinema.org

✉ Via Montebello 20

€ museum & panoramic lift combined ticket adult/concession €6.80/5.20

◷ 9am-8pm Tue-Fri & Sun, 9am-11pm Sat

ⓘ Information is available at the ticket office

▢ to Via Po

♿ good

✗ Sotto La Mole (p79)

Since 2000, the Mole has housed the equally riveting **Museo Nazionale del Cinema**. Split across five floors, it leads visitors on a fascinating interactive tour of Italian cinematic history – from its birth in Turin to

Installation (Asian shadowplay), Museo Nacionale di Cinema, Mole Antonelliana

Mole Antonelliana and another highlight of Turin

the present day – and is the only cinema museum in Italy. Love, death, horror and Turin are among the themes illustrated with movie clips in 10 chapels in the Temple Hall; in the 'love' chapel you lie on a bed of red, heart-shaped cushions to watch the movies, and in the 'humour' one you walk through an American fridge and sit on a toilet. If it's cinematic artefacts and curios you seek, then you'll be delighted by such oddities as Charlie Chaplin's bowler hat, and an enormous shark head from *Jaws*.

The upper levels of the museum feature an educational area covering the various stages of film-making, and an interesting poster gallery showing a small glimpse of the museum's 200,000-strong collection. If all that leaves you in need of a good lie down, then the rather sexy chaise longes in the impressive Temple Hall allow you to recline and view 35mm films in five-star style.

The museum is a particularly good spot to keep children entertained for hours on end, as it offers views, a space-age ride of sorts (see box), entertaining exhibits and a place to refuel.

A Cinematic Sight
The best view in the city can be had by ascending to the top of the heap ('mole' means just that in Italian) via the slick, futuristic elevator that whizzes visitors over 85m to the building's roof terrace in an impressive 59 seconds. The journey to the top will have cinema buffs recalling Fritz Lang's *Metropolis*. The stunning views take in the surrounding city and are equally breathtaking (and romantic) at night – although queues can be long on weekends and especially on Saturday night. If it's only the elevator you wish to take you can pay €3.60/2.60.

CASTELLO DI RIVOLI (2, B2)

One of the Savoy family's lavish residences (from the 14th century onwards), the Castello di Rivoli lies 17km to the west of central Turin in Rivoli. Architecturally the building owes a debt to numerous architects, from Carlo de Castellamonte to Filippo Juvarra, who all took part in the shaping of this imposing edifice, especially after it was obliterated by French troops commanded by General Nicolas de Catinat in 1693. In 1883, the property was sold by the Savoy family to the town of Rivoli, and it was used for various military purposes until the late 1970s. The **castle** now houses a stunning contemporary art gallery known as the **Museo d'Arte Contemporanea.** In the 1960s it was decided to restore the building, and a mix of architectural and restorative techniques means that the old and the new mingle in a way that allows people to see exactly what has been done throughout the complex. A stunningly successful refurbishment of the 17th-century wing known as the **Manica Lunga**

INFORMATION

- ☎ 011 956 52 22
- 🖳 www.castellodi
  rivoli.org
- ✉ Piazza Malfalda di
  Savoia, Rivoli
- € adult/concession/
  child €6.50/4.50/
  free
- 🕑 10am-5pm Tue-
  Thu, 10am-9pm
  Fri-Sun
- 🚌 36 to Rivoli then
  36/ to the castle
  from Rivoli (70
  minutes in all)
- 🅿 yes
- ♿ good
- 🍴 café & Combal.Zero
  (p72)

Modern art in a 14th-century castle

Castello di Rivoli, contemporary art gallery

('long sleeve') extends from the structure and contains an impressively proportioned gallery that seems flooded with light and houses temporary exhibits. It also contains a café, the fashionable Combal.Zero restaurant and the museum's well-stocked bookshop. The **permanent collection**, begun in 1984, is housed in the 'castello' proper and allows for the works of individual artists to be presented in a room each – don't be surprised though if certain lavish baroque features from the building's interior compete with some of the paintings, sculptures and installations that represent the modern era. Artists whose works feature in the permanent collection include (to name a few): Franz Ackermann, Giovanni Anselmo, Maurizio Cattelan (he of the dangling horse controversy), Francesco Clemente, Nan Goldin, Rebecca Horn, Per Kirkeby, Jeff Koons, Hain Steinbach and Wolfgang Tillmans.

The museum also presents a number of exhibitions each year featuring Italian and international artists and covering a wide range of styles from painting and sculpture to multimedia and photography.

DON'T MISS
- Catching sight of the mountain backdrop from vantage points around the property
- Refuelling with a coffee from the snazzy café
- Feasting your eyes on a temporary exhibition

PORTA PALAZZO MARKET (3, D5)

The liveliest place in Turin, the Porta Palazzo market hums with the activity of close to 700 stalls crammed with everything you ever wanted, vociferous vendors, bargain-hunting locals and more sights, sounds and smells than you can poke a stick at. It claims to be Europe's largest open-air market and sprawls around **Piazza della Repubblica**, a once-handsome Juvarra-designed square that fell on hard times and is thankfully being restored to its former glory.

INFORMATION

- 🖥 www.comune
  .torino.it/porta
  palazzo
- ✉ Piazza della
  Repubblica
- € free
- ⏰ 8.30am-1.30pm
  Mon-Fri, 8.30am-
  6.30pm Sat
- 🚌 🚃 to Porta
  Palazzo
- 🍴 hundreds of food
  stalls

Drive a bargain at Porta Palazzo

Despite its chaotic appearance, the layout of the market is reasonably straightforward. Its southwestern quadrant stocks lots of flowers, second-hand or discount clothing and the indoor seafood emporium, with more creatures from the deep than you thought possible to find in such a fresh state this far inland. Shifting over to the southeastern part of the market you'll find lots of fruit and vegetable stalls, plus a building that stocks a great array of deli produce – all perfect for stocking a picnic hamper. Across Corso Regina Margherita you'll find the lovely **Art-Nouveau building (1916)** that seems full to bursting with meats (including some cuts you didn't know were still being eaten) and cheeses. Just outside the building is a good spot to source cheap household goods and kitchen utensils, plus shoes. Across Corso Giulio Cesare is the **Massimiliano Fuksas–designed building** that will have replaced the old clothing market by the time you read this. It's a space-age addition to this historic area and part of the ongoing rejuvenation of this most engaging and multicultural quarter.

Changing Faces

The market is a great place to come face to face with the real Turin and its changes. It's a haunt for everyone, from bourgeois bargain hunters in their shopping finery, to southern and northeastern Italians from the wave of immigration in the 1960s and the newest of the newcomers from North Africa and eastern Europe. Prick up your ears – you're going to be hearing a lot of languages!

MUSEO EGIZIO (4, E4)

Considered to house one of the best collections of ancient Egyptian art outside of London and Cairo, the Museo Egizio (Egyptian Museum) is absolutely compelling. Based in the imposing **Palazzo dell'Accademia delle Scienze** since 1824, the museum's mammoth collection grew out of a bunch of antiquities Carlo Felice of Savoy purchased from a French consul in Egypt in 1824. Among its wealth of **recreated tombs** is that of pharaoh architect Kha and his wife Merit; the contents displayed (unearthed in 1906) were buried with them and are believed to date to 1400 BC. Expect to find incredibly well-preserved items from everyday Egyptian life, including wigs, garlic and other sundries. You'll also come across the **Ellesiya temple**, which was situated on the west bank of the Nile in Nubia (XVIII

INFORMATION
- ☎ 011 561 77 76
- 🖥 www.museoegizio .org, in Italian
- ✉ Via Accademia delle Scienze 6
- € €6.50/3, under 18 & over 65 free, combined ticket with Galleria Sabauda €8
- 🕐 8.30am-7.30pm Tue-Sun
- ℹ English-language signs
- 🚌 🚊 to Piazza Castello
- ♿ good

dynasty, New Kingdom) and features bas-reliefs and monumental statues. It was a gift from the Egyptian government for help on the Aswan Dam project. Closer to home, Turin-based relics that seem to pop up out of nowhere include fragments of the **original walls of Roman Turin**. Allow at least two hours to do the museum justice.

Slow Going

The museum is undergoing a painstakingly slow restoration programme, which means that visits can sometimes be hampered by a lack of staffing or room closures. Some rooms reveal progress, others none at all, but it's still well worth a visit, and things should be in better shape by 2006.

The Museo Egizio has the Ancient Egyptian art scene cornered

FONDAZIONE SANDRETTO RE REBAUDENGO (3, A8)

Nothing epitomises Turin's rejuvenation and love of contemporary art better than Fondazione Sandretto Re Rebaudengo, a 3500 sq-metre mother lode that combines the most noteworthy artworks with cutting-edge modern architecture and a fervent desire to bring modern art to the masses. As a result, you won't find this artistic gem in one of the posh neighbourhoods, but in the sometimes gritty San Paolo quarter, home of closed factories, dreary apartment blocks and ordinary shops and eateries. After an initially lukewarm reception from its neighbours, the Fondazione's exhibition space has been accepted and is now an important focal point within the community.

INFORMATION

- ☎ 011 1983 16 00
- 🖥 www.fondsrr.org
- ✉ Via Modane 16
- € €5/3, free under 12 & from 8pm Thu
- 🕐 noon-8pm Tue, Wed & Fri-Sun, noon-11pm Thu
- ℹ ticket office with English-language information & audio guides
- 🚌 58, 58/
- ♿ good
- 🍴 Spazio (p80)

The space, a minimalist, spare construction that spreads itself over a park, was designed by Claudio Silvestrin with engineer James Hardwick and features plenty of blindingly white walls and unobtrusive fittings, so that the art is what speaks to you loudest. Stellar **temporary exhibitions** follow thematic ideas – one of the most successful in recent times was the women-only roster of 2004 shows, among which was *Non Toccare La Donna Bianca* (Don't Touch The White Woman), which featured works from women artists from around the world.

DON'T MISS
- Eating at Spazio (p80)
- Perusing the arty tomes in the bookshop
- Popping in for *aperitivo* hour after 8pm on Thursday, when entry is free and the museum bar is jumping

Step up to some challenging contemporary art at Fondazione Sandretto Re Rebaudengo

BASILICA DI SUPERGA (2, E2)

The city of Turin found itself besieged by the Spanish and French armies in 1706, motivating Vittorio Amedeo II to pledge that if the city was saved he would build a basilica to honour the Virgin Mary. When the city was duly saved, renowned architect Filippo Juvarra was called upon to design the Basilica Superga on a hill about 10km northeast of Central Turin. A glorious baroque edifice with a **double canopied dome** in the style of St Peter's in Vatican City (but smaller), the edifice serves as a place of worship and the final resting spot of the Savoys. The lavish **tombs** of Turin's noble family make for interesting viewing, as does the heart-starting ascent to the *cupola* (dome).

On the night of 4 May 1949, the basilica became another tomb of sorts, when the plane carrying the Grande Torino football team crashed into the rear base of the basilica in thick fog after a match in Portugal. The entire playing team and various support staff were killed in the tragedy, with 31 dead and the city of Turin in mourning. The site is commemorated with a simple **shrine** at the back, and still receives plenty of floral tributes from local fans of the team.

INFORMATION

☎ 011 898 00 83

✉ Strada della Basilica di Superga 73

€ €5 for dome and tombs

☼ basilica 9am-noon & 3-6pm Apr-Oct, 9am-noon 3-5pm Nov-Mar; cupola 9.30am-noon & 3-6pm Mon-Fri, 9.30am-7.30pm Sat, 1-7.30pm Sun Apr-Oct, 9.30am-6.30pm Sat & 1-6.30pm Sun Nov-Mar; tombs 9.30am-1.30pm & 2.30-6.30pm Mon-Fri, 9.30am-7.30pm Sat & Sun Apr-Oct, 9.30am-1.30pm & 2.30-6.30pm Sat & Sun Nov-Mar

🚊 🚌 tram 15, then *tranvia* from Stazione Sassi or bus 79

P yes

♿ limited

✕ Pizzeria Stazione Sassi (p82)

Sassy Stazione Sassi

To get to Superga, take tram No 15 from Piazza Castello to the Sassi-Superga stop on Corso Casale, then walk 20m to **Stazione Sassi** (☎ 800 01 91 52; Strada Communale di Superga 4; Mon-Fri €3.10/1.55, Sat, Sun & hols €4.15/2.60; ☼ 9am-noon & 2-8pm Mon & Wed-Fri, 7am-midnight Tue, 9am-8pm Sat, Sun & hols), the cable-car station from where an original tram dating from 1934 rattles the 3.1km route up the hillside (18 minutes, hourly). In winter, consideration is shown to its passengers with heating underneath the slatted wooden seats! Getting there is half the fun it seems…

PINACOTECA GIOVANNI E MARELLA AGNELLI (6, A4)

INFORMATION
- ☎ 011 006 20 08
- 🖳 www.pinacoteca
  -agnelli.it
- ✉ Via Nizza 230
- € €4/2.50
- 🕒 10am-7pm Tue-Sun
- ℹ multilingual audio
  guides
- 🚌 🚊 bus 1, 35,
  tram 18
- P yes
- ♿ good
- ✕ La Pista (p81)

What better way to put a cherry on top of a wildly successful factory refurbishment than with a jewel box (hence the nickname **lo Scrigno**) of an art gallery that displays a few dozen gems from the former factory owner's dazzling private collection? The Pinacoteca Giovanni e Marella Agnelli features, among its 18th- to 20th-century works, a series of early sketches made for FIAT advertisements. The better-known pieces among the small but judicious collection include some beautiful 18th-century pieces by **Canaletto**, a wonderful assortment of **Matisse** paintings and the striking *Nu Couché* by **Amedeo Modigliani**. Architecture buffs will revel in the Renzo Piano–designed gallery, which features extraordinary technical touches that allow light to infuse the space without damaging the artworks, and you'll also be able to enjoy grand views over the city and to **La Bolla**, which also shares the roof here. Note that it was here, in lo Scrigno, that Giovanni Agnelli's coffin was placed before his funeral.

DON'T MISS
- Taking a turn on the rooftop car-testing track after a turn in the gallery – the views are fabulous
- Buying some glossy books from the well-stocked on-site bookshop

Possibly the only jewellery box in the world with a helipad for a lid

GALLERIA CIVICA D'ARTE MODERNA E CONTEMPORANEA (GAM; 4, A6)

The agenda is set before you even walk in the door: 'All Art Has Been Contemporary' is proclaimed in electric blue from the roof of this excellent art museum. It comprises a 20,000-strong collection, of which about 600 works from the 19th, 20th and 21st century are on display at any given time. The collection starts on the 2nd floor with works from the 19th century, including many from regional artists such as **Luigi Baldassare Reviglio**, whose landscapes of Turin (1809–32) are a good indication of artistic themes of the time. If you want a better idea of what the city looked like in the mid-19th century, then visit **Carlo Bossoli's** paintings, which depict recognisable Turin landmarks.

On the 1st floor major works of the 20th century by both Italian and foreign artists are arranged by themes such as Art in Turin between the Two World Wars. Important works by artists such as **Picabia**, **Calder**, **Chillida**, **Twombly**, **Picasso**, **Ernst**, **Klee**, **Warhol** and **Jørn** mingle with pieces from Torinese artists such as the extraordinary **Carol Rama**, **Piero Ruggeri**, **Aldo Mondino** and **Piero Gilardi**. Give yourself a couple of hours to take in the collection, more if you want to peruse any of the temporary exhibitions, which in recent times have included some of the thought-provoking installations of Milan-based duo **Vedovamazzei** (who parked a truck filled with water outside the museum in 2004). Get ready to make use of the Philippe Starck chairs that provide welcome relief.

INFORMATION
- ☎ 011 562 99 11
- 🖥 www.gamtorino.it
- ✉ Via Magenta 31
- € €5.50/3
- ⏱ 9am-7pm Tue-Sun
- 🚌 1, 64
- ♿ good
- ☕ café

Cutting-edge Sculpture at Galleria Civica d'Arte Moderna e Contemporanea

DON'T MISS
- Any of Turin-born Medardo Rosso's sculptures
- Giorgio de Chirico's *Self Portrait*
- Carol Rama's *Ricordati di quegli anni e li fa schizza via*

GALLERIA SABAUDA (4, E4)

Housed in the same palazzo that holds the magnificent Museo Egizio, this is a fine way to finish off a big day of sights. It represents one of the most important art collections in the region – that of the dukes and kings of Savoy, and the gallery was established

DON'T MISS
- Orazio Gentileschi's *Annunciation*
- Maria Giovanna Clemente's *Portrait of Carlo Emanuele III*
- Guercino's *The Prodigal Son*

by Carlo Alberto in 1832 (the collection has been displayed here since 1865). It's a wonderful showcase of 14th to 19th century Piedmontese, Italian and Flemish painters,

INFORMATION
- ☎ 011 547 440
- 🖳 www.museitorino .it/galleriasabauda, in Italian
- ✉ Via Accademia delle Scienze 6
- € adult/concession €4/2, combined ticket with Museo Egizio €8, under 18 & over 65 free
- 🕐 8.30am-2pm Tue & Fri-Sun, 2.30-7.30pm Wed & Thu
- 🚌 🚊 to Piazza Castello
- ♿ limited

and is arranged in order of the collectors, rather than by chronology or theme. Artists of note whose works can be found in the collection include **Mantegna**, **Van Eyck**, **Memling**, **Rembrandt**, **Van Dyck**, **Bronzino** and **Botticelli**, plus numerous artists' attempts to capture the Savoys in the most flattering light. Variations on this last theme are the fabulous battle scenes painted for Eugene of Savoy by **Jan van Huchtenburg**. English-language descriptions of the artworks can be found on laminated cards in various rooms.

Culture this way...

PALAZZO REALE (4, F2)

Statues of Roman deities **Castor and Pollux** flank the entrance to Turin's Palazzo Reale (Royal Palace), which was the Savoy family home until 1865 and is an outwardly austere building erected for Carlo Emanuele II around 1646. Inside, the austerity disappears, revealing lavishly decorated rooms, connected to the entrance hall by Filippo Juvarra's celebrated **Scala delle Forbici** (literally, 'staircase of scissors'), an engineering feat and artistic marvel given the space constraints. The palace, which insists upon a rather lacklustre guided tour (Italian only) is nevertheless a great place to understand changes in aesthetic taste over 200 years and view past trends in royal decoration. Rooms that warrant close attention include the over-the-top **Throne Room** with its gilded wooden ceiling, the **Chinese Room** (no palace should be without one it would seem), with its panels sourced by Juvarra and others made in Turin by Pietro Massa, plus the extraordinary **Dining Room**, with its table set as if waiting for guests.

INFORMATION
- ☎ 011 436 14 55
- 🖥 www.ambienteto.arti.beniculturali.it, in Italian
- ✉ Piazza Castello
- € adult/concession €6.50/3.25, under 18 & over 65 free
- 🕙 9am-7pm Tue-Sun
- ⓘ compulsory guided tour (in Italian), printed English-language explanations
- 🚌 🚊 to Piazza Castello
- ♿ limited

Black Meets White
The dividing line between the black-and white-magic halves of the city (p41) passes through the space between the statues of Castor and Pollux outside the Palazzo Reale.

Shuttered inside the Palazzo Reale is the famous staircase of scissors

PALAZZO MADAMA   (4, F3)

This part-medieval, part-baroque castle dominates the square. Built in the 13th century on the site of the old Roman gate, it gained its name as the 17th-century residence of Madama Reale Maria Cristina, the widow of Vittorio Amedeo I. Its rich, baroque façade was added later by Juvarra between 1718 and 1721. Over the centuries it has served as a prison, barracks, royal cellar, senate and court. Its curious appearance means that from the front or from the back the building looks completely different. During Luci d'Artista (see p84), a narrative by North American artist Jenny Holzer is projected onto the 'back wall'.

INFORMATION

☎ 011 442 99 12
✉ Piazza Castello
€ free
🕒 10am-8pm Tue-Fri & Sun, 10am-11pm Sat
🚌 🚊 bus 55, 56, 68, tram 13, 15, 18
♿ limited

Recently reopened, at least in part, you can now visit Juvarra's **grand staircase** and the **Voltone room** and **great hall** was slated to be ready by 2005. Archaeological excavations can be viewed from the Voltone room.

The **Museo Civico d'Arte Antica**, which is also housed in the palace, displays paintings and sculptures by Piedmontese artists from the medieval period to the 17th century. At time of research it was due to reopen in time for the winter Olympics in 2006.

Skirting the Issue

One of the reasons that Palazzo Madama underwent extensive remodelling in the 18th century was to accommodate the wide skirts of ladies' fashions of the time. It seemed that a wider, more generously proportioned staircase was deemed a fashion essential, and Filippo Juvarra was just the man for the job.

The very grand and well-watered Palazzo Madama

PALAZZINA DI CACCIA DI STUPINIGI (2, C3)

Pack your camera for this one – people will actually want to see these happy snaps from your trip. The Savoys' sprawling hunting lodge, known as Stupinigi for short, lies in manicured grounds beyond FIAT's monstrous Mirafiori complex. A Juvarra creation and world-famous rococo delight, the building was designed for Vittorio Amedeo II in 1729 (as a replacement for Reggia Venaria Reale – see p32). Many parts of the building are in their original condition (and therefore extremely fragile – please don't take photos of the decaying interior). The whole pile is being slowly

INFORMATION
- ☎ 011 358 12 20
- 💻 pstorico@
  mauriziano.it
- ✉ Piazza Principe
  Amedeo 7
- € €6.20/5.20
- ⏲ 10am-6pm Tue-Sun
  Apr-Oct, 9am-5pm
  Tue-Sun Nov-Mar
- ℹ small bookshop on
  site
- 🚋 🚌 tram 4, then
  bus 41
- P yes
- ♿ limited

and painstakingly restored with a ton of FIAT money, but you'll still get the feeling (especially when there are few visitors) that you've stumbled upon

DON'T MISS
- Catching sight of the giant iron stag that sits atop the building
- Getting a closer look at the copper original that sits in the ticket office
- Spotting the Juvarra-designed farm cottages that line the approach to the palace

an abandoned palace as you wander through elaborately decorated rooms to the showstopper that is Juvarra's extraordinary **Salone Centrale**, with its incredible chandelier. The whole experience comes under the banner of the **Museo di Arte e Ammobiliamento**, a collection of art and furniture from Savoy palaces (that frankly, should be better looked after security-wise).

The substantial and stunning Palazzina di Caccia di Stupinigi

DUOMO DI SAN GIOVANNI BATTISTA (4, F2)

Built between 1491 and 1498 on the site of three 14th-century basilicas, Turin's cathedral is the city's only remaining example of Renaissance architecture (it has a façade typical of the Florentine style). But that's not why thousands upon thousands of people come here each year. It also happens to be the home of Christendom's most controversial cloth – the **Holy Shroud of Turin**, a copy of which is on permanent display in front of the cathedral altar, resting flat in a vacuum-sealed box stored in a controlled atmosphere. In the past it was housed in the **Capella della Santa Sindone** (1668–94), which was designed by noted architect Guarino Guarini. In 1997 the cappella was seriously damaged by fire, and is currently undergoing restoration.

INFORMATION
- ☎ 011 436 15 40
- ✉ Piazza San Giovanni
- € free
- ⏲ 7am-12.30pm & 3-7pm Mon-Sat, 8am-12.30pm & 3-7pm Sun
- ⓘ volunteer guides on site
- 🚌 🚋 to Porta Palazzo
- ♿ good

Marble shrouds the *duomo*

DON'T MISS
- The Romanesque bell tower, designed by Juvarra and built from 1720 to 1723
- The Capella di Santi Crispino e Crispiniano – the patron saints of cobblers
- The replica of the *Last Supper* above the main door

If you want to see the real shroud, you're in for a long wait – it's only displayed every 25 years or so, and the next scheduled appearance is 2025. That said, the large replica will give you a good enough idea of what Christ's supposed burial cassock looks like, and volunteer guides are always keen to explain why they believe it's the genuine article. If you're not a keen shroudie, rest assured, the simple cruciform interior with charming trompe l'oeil painted details is reason enough to visit.

MUSEO DELLA SINDONE (MUSEUM OF THE SHROUD) (3, C5)

For centuries experts and fanatics have argued over the authenticity of the Holy Shroud of Turin, said to be the burial cloth in which Jesus' body was wrapped after the crucifixion. How the image of a human body – with fractured nose, bruised right cheek, lance wound on chest, scourge marks on back, thorn wounds on forehead and nail wounds on both wrists and feet – was formed on the cloth remains the biggest mystery.

Crusaders first brought the shroud to Europe. It belonged to Louis of Savoy from 1453 who folded the cloth into squares and stashed it in a silver treasure trove in Chambéry in France. The tie dye–style brown patterns visible on it today were caused by a fire in 1532 that saw a drop of hot silver fall into the casket and through the folded layers.

In 1578 the sacred Holy Shroud was brought from Chambéry to Turin. The shroud had already been moved to the region for safe-keeping twice before – during the 1533 French invasion of Savoy, and again during the Italian Wars. Both times the cloth was hidden in the Cattedrale di Sant'Eusebio in Vercelli.

INFORMATION
- ☎ 011 436 58 32
- 🖳 www.sindone.it, in Italian
- ✉ Via San Domenico 28
- € €5.50/2.20
- 🕑 9am-noon & 3-7pm
- ℹ multilingual headsets
- 🚌 🚊 to Porta Palazzo
- ♿ good

Medieval mixup or sacred shroud?

Tests in 1981 uncovered traces of human blood and pollen from plants known to exist only around Jerusalem. Many guessed the shroud dated from AD 1260 to 1390; carbon dating tests carried out in 1988 seemed to confirm this, tying it to the 13th century and making it far from sacred. Most agree that the white cloth – 4.37m long and 1.10m wide – was woven in the Middle East.

Shroud fiends shouldn't overlook the Museo della Sindone, which, despite its displays and shroud **paraphernalia**, does little to answer the major unanswered questions. Guided tours are in Italian only; ask for a free English-language audio guide. An interesting **multilingual film** is also available for viewing.

Shrouded in Mystery

Some theorists have posited that the Shroud is actually the first-ever attempt at photography (using a camera obscura) by Leonardo da Vinci. Mind you, there's no real proof that makes this more likely than the other big theory…

MUSEO DI ANTICHITÀ (4, F1)

Housed in the former orangeries of the Royal Gardens, this collection of 7000 years of antiquities from the region of Piedmont won't do much to illuminate your sense of history if you don't read Italian, but it is interesting nonetheless. Exhibits cover the Palaeolithic era to the Middle Ages, but also wonder into thematic territory such as *La Tavola e La Cucina* (The Table and the Kitchen). You'll also see some fine examples of **Greek and Roman sculpture**, **Etruscan and Cypriot ceramics** and a rather lacklustre (when we visited anyway – it may well have since improved) assortment of statues grouped together under some sort of Olympic theme.

DON'T MISS
- The mosaics of Orpheus (3rd century AD)
- The bronze Minerva (2nd century AD)
- The collection of red and black vases

INFORMATION
- ☎ 011 521 11 06
- 🖳 www.museoantichita.it, In Italian
- ✉ Via XX Settembre 88c
- € €4/2
- 🕙 8.30am-7.30pm Tue-Sun
- 🚌 🚈 to Porta Palazzo
- ♿ good

Our tip for an excursion to this area is to also visit the Roman Anfiteatro, located between the duomo and the Museo di Antichità, and be sure to also check out the Porta Palatina nearby. Both are terrific examples of the Roman settlement and will enhance the experience.

The Museo di Antichita covers 7000 years of antiquities. You can do it in a day..

MUSEO NAZIONALE DEL RISORGIMENTO   (4, F4)

Italy's first short-lived parliament in Turin forms part of the interesting Museo Nazionale del Risorgimento, which has extensive displays of arms, paintings and documents tracing the turbulent history of the region and of what came to be a unified Italy from 1706 (the Battle of Turin) to WWII. You'll travel through time from the Enlightenment, Napoleonic rule, the 1848 insurrection and the Crimean War to the achievement of Unity, all housed in large-scale rooms with little in the way of English explanations. If you're not such a keen history boffin, then you may just want to content yourself with Palazzo Carignano's robust red-brick exterior, embellished with plenty

INFORMATION
- ☎ 011 562 11 47
- 🖳 www.regione .piemonte.it/cul tura/risorgimento
- ✉ Palazzo Carignano, Via Accademia delle Scienze 5
- € €5/3.50
- ⏱ 10am-7pm
- 🚌 🚋 to Piazza Castello
- ♿ good, some Braille explanations

of stars, designed by Guarino Guarini for Prince Emanuele Filiberto in the 17th century. Don't miss seeing the elliptical **Hall of the Subalpine Parliament**, which stands as it was left for its last session in 1860.

Baby Steps

Vittorio Emanuele II, Italy's first king, was born in the baroque **Palazzo Carignano**. It was here that the Chamber of Deputies of the Kingdom of Sardinia met (1848–60) and where Italy's first parliament sat between 1861 and 1864 (until the capital was moved to Florence).

Bithplace of the Italian nation — Museo Nazionale del Risorgimento

PALAZZO BRICHERASIO (4, E5)

INFORMATION
- ☎ 011 571 18 11
- 💻 www.palazzo bricherasio.it, in Italian
- ✉ Via Lagrange 20
- € adult/concession/ child €7/5/3.50
- 🕑 2.30-7.30pm Mon, 9.30am-7.30pm Tue, Wed & Fri, 9.30am-10.30pm Thu & Sat
- ℹ audio guide s/d €3/4.50
- 🚌 🚋 🚎 to Porta Nuova
- 🅿 pay car park nearby
- ♿ good

A 17th-century palace that has been admirably restored houses one of the city's best art museums, specialising mostly in modern art but not averse to special exhibitions of past masters. Inside, you'll find a thoughtfully planned space that makes excellent use of the palace's proportions and features, but makes no bones about the fact that certain modern details were required to make the space 'work'. To whit, the stunning ovoid-shaped glass elevator that pierces the centre of the gallery, and the glass and steel spiral staircase entwined around it. The **modern art** often contrasts nicely with the exquisite **baroque features** of the palace, such as the elaborate ceilings or the grand staircase that initially takes you to the viewing rooms – and that doesn't mean that only the interior highlights this blend of the old and new. The building has been 'wrapped' by Cristo, and in 2004–05 giant see-through bubbles were poised to escape from the windows near the entrance (they were part of Loris Cecchini's 'blaublobbing' exhibit) – bringing some of the most exciting installations out into the open.

Signed, Sealed & Delivered
Apart from being the residence of assorted nobles over the years, Palazzo Bricherasio also played a small part in local history when the documents that established FIAT were signed here on 1 July 1899.

Blaublobbing at Palazzo Bricherasio

PALAZZO CAVOUR   (4, E5)

A confirmed fan of Turin's café culture, Count Camillo Benso di Cavour, the architect of Italian unification, was born and died in Palazzo Cavour, a baroque palace dating to 1729. It can be visited during temporary exhibitions held in its spacious and grandiose interior, which has undergone some sensitive renovations over the years and is worth visiting. The building, one of the city's strongest examples of the 18th-century Piedmont Baroque style, was commissioned by Count Michel Antonio di Cavour (the grandfather of Count Camillo), with Giovanni Giacomo Planteri (1680–1756) as architect. Stunning rooms to take note of include the **'White Room'** and the **Sala Magnifica**, which are both accessible during exhibitions.

INFORMATION
- ☎ 011 53 06 90
- ✉ Via Cavour 8
- € €6.20/4.20
- ⏰ exhibitions 10am-7.30pm Tue, Wed & Fri-Sun, 10am-10pm Thu
- ⓘ guided tours available (booking required)
- 🚌 🚊 to Porta Nuova
- Ⓟ pay car park nearby
- ♿ good

Counting Cafés

History buffs who wish to venture a little further into a true Cavour itinerary will do well to frequent the following places in Turin: Ristorante del Cambio (p70), Caffé Fiorio (p74), Baratti & Milano (p85), Al Bicerin (p84) and Pasticceria Fratelli Stratta (p62). All are within rolling distance of Palazzo Cavour, and all are worth spending some time in sampling food, coffee and sweets.

A great place for Cavourting around

The Winter Olympics

For 17 days in 2006, all eyes will be on Piedmont and its capital Turin. As host to the XX Winter Olympic Games (10–26 February 2006) and IX Paralympic Winter Games (10–19 March 2006), the regional capital and its mountainous surrounds will host more than one million spectators, who will descend on this winter wonderland to watch people in all manner of outlandish outfits fight for supremacy over the elements and each other.

Preparations

Places on the Piedmont podium will be fought for at seven competition sites in the region, Turin serving as the springboard to a clutch of snow-covered mountain resorts in the Western Alps, where the sporting action will take place. Potential venue hiccups have been scouted out by a series of test events during 2004 and 2005: the Alpine World Ski Championships; the European figure-skating championships; the Six Nations ice-hockey tournament and so on.

The city's airport got a €98 million facelift, and during the Games competitors will live in purpose-built Olympic villages in Turin, Bardonecchia and Sestriere. The 70,000 sq-metre Turin village, in the Lingotto district, will be kitted out with a canteen, shopping mall, recreation areas, medical centre and massage facilities, as well as accommodation for 2500 aspiring medallists. Solar panels are among bio-architectural features destined for the state-of-the-art complex which, after the Games, will become residential housing and a research centre.

And on top of all that, the city put old railway lines underground and built a brand-new Metro system to improve access to the sites and around the city.

Events

Today's athletes vie for gold in almost 100 different skiing (downhill, cross-country and jumping), skating, sledding and snowboarding events. They are, in alphabetical order: Alpine skiing, biathlon, bobsleigh, cross-country skiing, curling, figure skating, freestyle, ice hockey, luge, Nordic combined, short track, skeleton, ski jumping, snowboard and speed skating.

Turin's Olympic Venues

Turin will host Olympic ice-hockey, speed-skating, figure-skating and short-track events. The Olympic District will host the **Olympic Village**, **Media Centre** and **Lingotto Oval**, a new speed-skating palace big enough to hold 8200 spectators and four football pitches. After the Games, the €58 million building will become an exhibition space.

Figure- and short-track skaters will compete at the **Palavela**, the iconic 1960s building that has been revamped by architect Gae Aulenti. Hockey players will battle it out for gold in front of 6000 fans on a temporary rink in **Torino Esposizioni** and in the **Palasport Olimpico**, a steely new stadium designed by Tokyo-based architect Arata Isozakj. Turin's 1930s **Stadio Comunale**, a football stadium that's been closed since 1990, is in line for an Olympic makeover as host to the opening and closing ceremonies.

Getting Tickets

Tickets went on sale in November 2004. Prices vary depending on the event, with single-event tickets costing anything from €20 (curling) to €170 (ski jumping). That said, half of the million tickets on sale cost €50 or less. Buy them online through http://torino2006.ticketone.it; in Italy at TicketOne sales points (including FNAC in Turin) or branches of the Sanpaolo bank; and through National Olympic Committees in other countries. Tickets will be allocated by lottery 45 days after they go on sale.

The Maestro

Watched by an expected audience of 35,000 in the stadium and two billion TV spectators worldwide, the opening and closing ceremonies in Stadio Comunale will be as much a celebration of Italian culture as of Olympic tradition. We spoke with Ric Birch, the visionary and producer of the events:

What in particular excites you about Turin?
In Milan, the feeling there is that Turin is *the* place for up-and-coming designs and ideas, for young ideas. Turin is really seen as a city of the future.

What differences are there between the Winter and Summer Olympics?
Well, the biggest difference is that you really have to get out of town to experience the Winter games – the big ceremonies will be held in Turin, but largely it will be the administrative centre of the games. Winter games are more widespread, geographically speaking.

How do you strike a balance between what's televisual and what's good for the stadium audience?
I'm glad you asked! It has got to be successful for the people sitting in the stadium first and foremost, because if it's good for them, then TV rocks along with it. It can't be done the other way because you end up with a stony silence in the stadium that's obvious to the people watching on TV.

Is there a formula for working on events of this scale?
Well, there's no creative formula, but there is a formula in terms of infrastructure. The formula's for organising, not creating. Luckily, we never get the feeling that the technology can't keep up with our ideas – these events are always at the forefront of it all.

How many volunteers will you have for the ceremonies?
About 2000 backstage volunteers and about 5000 performers, plus a show crew of between 150 and 200.

What if it snows?
In Turin, it's more likely to be foggy…

Sights & Activities

MUSEUMS

Archivio di Stato (4, F3)

Under the porticoes in Piazza Castello's northeastern corner you'll find the State Archives which, together with a **second State Archives site** (Via Piave 21), holds documentation from 13 centuries stored on 70km of shelves. Its oldest document goes back to AD 726, and the building was designed by Filippo Juvarra.
☎ 011 562 46 10
✉ Piazza Castello 209
€ free ☼ 9am-5.45pm Mon-Fri, 9am-1.45pm Sat
🚌 🚃 to Piazza Castello

Armeria Reale (4, F2)

The Savoys were great collectors of art, but they were also a well-armed bunch, as you'll see in the Royal Armoury, which has recently undergone a restoration. Hidden under the porticoes just to the right of the Palazzo Madama gates, it contains what some claim to be Europe's best collection of daggers, guns and assorted killing instruments.
☎ 011 54 38 89
🖥 www.artito.arti
.beniculturali.it, Italian only ✉ Piazza Castello 191 € €2/free
☼ 8.30am-2pm Mon, Wed & Fri, 1.30-7.30pm Thu, Sat & Sun 🚌 🚃 to Piazza Castello

Biblioteca Reale (4, F2)

Adjoining the Armeria Reale, the Royal Library dates back to 1831, has more than 200,000 volumes, 5000 16th-century books, several thousand manuscripts and a famous self-portrait scribbled in crayon by none other than Leonardo da Vinci. It's a stunningly beautiful space, so make time for it.
☎ 011 45 38 55 ✉ Piazza Castello 191 € free
☼ 8.45am-6.45pm Mon, Wed & Fri, 8.30am-1.30pm Tue, Thu & Sat
🚌 🚃 to Piazza Castello

Museo Civico Pietro Micca (3, B6)

Turin was beseiged by the French in 1706 — and all the drama is captured in this interesting museum named after the hero of the four-month siege. Detailed captions in English outline French attacks on other fortresses in the Duchy of Savoy and there's a scale model of Turin before the siege. The highlight is a guided tour by torchlight of a 300m section of the defensive tunnels running beneath the city. At the time of research the museum was opening and closing its doors on a regular basis — check with the tourist offices to see if it's open when you visit.
☎ 011 54 63 17 ✉ Via Guicciardini 7 € €3/2
☼ 9am-7pm Tue-Sun
🚌 🚃 🚃 to Porta Susa

Museo dell'Automobile (6, C4)

Among the hundreds of automotive masterpieces in this rather dilapidated Soviet-style building is one of the first ever FIATs, and the Isotta Fraschini driven by Gloria Swanson in the film *Sunset Boulevard*. There are explanations in English throughout the museum.
☎ 011 67 76 66
🖥 www.museoauto.it,

See one of the first FIATs at the Museo dell'Automobile

Captivating Cappuccini

From Piazza Gran Madre di Dio, a road spirals up Monte dei Cappuccini (284m), used as a defensive outpost since Roman times. Carlo Emanuele I destroyed its previous fortification in 1583 to build the **Chiesa e Convento di Santa Maria** (5, F1). From the front terrace there's sweeping views of Turin and the Alps.

Italian only ⊠ Corso Unità d'Italia 40 € €5.50/4 🕑 10am-6.30pm Tue, Wed, Fri & Sat, 10am-10pm Fri, 10am-8.30pm Sun 🚌 34 🚻 good

Museo di Arti Decorative (4, H5)

The late antiques dealer Pietro Accorsi left this impressive collection of furniture and furnishings to the region, and it's well worth a visit. The rooms of this former palace are filled with interesting objects both great and small, from snuff boxes to elaborate commodes, and some wonderful hunting scenes by Cignaroli. As you'd expect, there are some wonderful examples of the 18th-century craze for 'Chinese' rooms. Guided tours are compulsory and usually in Italian, although printed information in English is supplied. ☎ 011 812 91 16 🖥 www.fondazioneaccorsi.it ⊠ Via Po 55 € €6.50/5 🕑 10am-8pm Tue, Wed & Fri-Sun, 10am-11pm Thu 🚌 🚋 to Via Po 🚻 good

Museo Nazionale della Montagna (5, F1)

One wing of the 17th-century convent of Santa Maria now shelters this museum founded by the Club Alpino Italiano (CAI) in 1877. Exhibits focus on Alpine flora and fauna, as well as man's meddling with mountains and his attempts to scale the world's peaks. At the time of writing, the permanent collection was closed to the public for restoration, and the entrance for temporary exhibits was at Via Giardino 48. ☎ 011 660 41 04 🖥 www.museomontagna.org ⊠ Via Giardino 39 € €5/3.50 🕑 9am-7pm 🚌 53, 55, 56, 66 🚻 good

Museo Regionale di Scienze Naturale (4, G5)

An Alaskan brown bear personally welcomes visitors to this animal-stuffed museum inside the eastern wing of a monumental 17th-century hospital with four inner courtyards and a chapel. It's a rather fusty, dusty collection, and a bit of a relic, but children seem to enjoy spending time here, and its popular with school groups, which livens things up somewhat. ☎ 011 4320 73 32 🖥 www.regione.piemonte.it/museoscienze naturali, Italian only ⊠ Via Giovanni Giolitti 36 € €5/2.50, under 18

free 🕑 10am-7pm Wed-Mon 🚌 🚋 to Via Po & Porta Nuova 🚻 good

Museo Storico Nazionale d'Artiglieria (4, B3)

This museum of weaponry and military memorabilia was closed for restoration at the time of writing, but should be open by the time you read this. It's housed in the *cittadella* (citadel), a mighty star-shaped structure built by Emanuele Filiberto after the city's liberation from the French in 1563, and boasts an 11,500-piece collection. Call first for opening times and prices. ☎ 011 562 92 23 🖥 www.artiglieria.org ⊠ Corso Galileo Ferraris 0 🚌 to Via Cernaia

Pinacoteca dell'Accademia Albertina di Belle Arti (4, G4)

This often-overlooked art gallery has over 300 works in its collection and some interesting copies of major works by artists such as Raffaello and Caravaggio, plus originals such as Bartolomeo Cavarozzi's skilful *Sacra Famiglia* (17th century) and Ludovico Raymond's over-the-top *Sacrilegio* (1881). It's on the 2nd floor of the building: you'll need to press the doorbell to gain entry. ☎ 011 817 78 62 🖥 www.accademialbertina.torino.it, Italian only ⊠ Via Accademia Albertina 8 € €4/2.60 🕑 9am-1pm & 3-7pm Tue-Sun 🚌 🚋 to Piazza Castello 🚻 good

ROYAL RESIDENCES

Some of the city's grand buildings may not be doing royal service any more, but they can sometimes be visited and are a wonderful part of the area's cultural heritage that's finally being recognised as a major attraction.

Castello de la Mandria

The Savoy family used to graze their horses on the land surrounding this royal retreat in Venaria. Standing at the heart of the 6500-hectare estate, the 18th-century castle was restored in the mid-19th century as a country hideaway for Vittorio Emanuele II and his lover, la Bela Rusin. Today, you can visit the spookily dilapidated royal apartments as well as enjoy the vast park, which is the largest wooded area in the Po Valley and features wild deer and boar that roam freely.

☎ 011 499 33 22
✉ Viale Carlo Emanuele II 256 € €6/3 ☽ by appointment only 🚌 72, then 1km walk

Castello del Valentino (5, C3)

Walking southwest along the River Po brings you to the 17th-century Castello del Valentino, a mock French-style chateau where Maria Cristina and Vittorio Amedeo I indulged in their courtly frolics. Technically, the building is closed to the public, but as it currently houses the architectural faculty of Turin polytechnic, it is possible to surreptitiously have a wander around the building and surrounds.

☎ 011 669 45 92
✉ Corso Massimo d'Azeglio 🚋 9, 16

Castello di Moncalieri (2, D3)

As a setting for police barracks, this imposing castle 7km south of Turin takes some beating. Dating from the 12th century, it was given an extensive makeover in the mid-17th century by Castellamonte, Juvarra and Alfieri. This imposing castle today houses a Carabinieri barracks, and contains a number of royal apartments that are open to the public; look for the Salotto Reale (Royal Drawing Room), the Salotto degli Specchi (Mirror Room) and the regal lavatories of Queen Maria Adelaide, wife of Vittorio Emanuele II.

☎ 011 64 13 03
✉ Piazza Baden Baden, Moncalieri € €2
☽ 9.30am-12.30pm & 2.15-6pm Thu, Sat & Sun 🚆 from Lingotto

Reggia Venaria Reale (2, C1)

Known as the Versailles of Italy, this massive castle (built in 1682) is in Venaria Reale, about 5km northwest of Turin, and was almost destroyed due to neglect and vandalism by the 1970s. Commissioned by Carlo Emanuele II in 1658, it was originally designed by Amedeo Castellamante and later worked on by Filippo Juvarra. His magnificent Galleria di Diana and Cappella di Sant'Uberto are but two justifiably celebrated highlights and, at the time of writing, the entire complex was undergoing extensive and impressive restoration work.

☎ 011 459 36 75
🖳 www.lavenariareale.it ✉ Piazza della Repubblica 4 € €5/3 ☽ by appointment only 🚌 72, then 1km walk

Castello Valentino is pretty impressive – we're not lyin'

ART GALLERIES

Turin's thriving contemporary art scene is reason enough to visit the city, and there are literally dozens of galleries that hold regular exhibitions and specialise in local artists. Pick up a copy of the brochure *artshow.it* (free) from art galleries to see listings of exhibitions and events in Turin.

Carlina (4, G5)
This small gallery on Piazza Carlina (as it's generally known) features modern artworks by Italian and foreign artists, such as Alighiero Boetti.
☎ 011 817 33 44
✉ Piazza Carlo Emanuele II 17a € free
⏱ 10.30am-12.30pm & 4-7.30pm Tue-Sat
🚌 🚋 to Piazza Castello

Davico
Davico is an attractive, subdued space in the lovely Galleria Subalpina (4, F3) and specialises in the more conservative, less out-there art market. Press the buzzer to enter a refined, handsome gallery and view small-scale themed exhibitions.
☎ 011 562 91 52
✉ Galleria Subalpina 30 € free ⏱ 10am-12.30pm & 4-7.30pm Tue-Sat 🚌 🚋 to Piazza Castello

Franco Noero (4, H6)
Worth visiting if only to start an argument with your most reactionary pal – recent exhibitions that stopped pedestrian traffic included Gabriel Kuri's eye-catching (and rather hypnotic) *Untitled (trinity)* of refrigerators with plastic bags hovering inside. Easily one of the best agenda-setting galleries in town, with installation work a particular strength.
☎ 011 88 22 08 🖥 www.franconoero.com ✉ Via Giovanni Giolitti 52a
€ free ⏱ 3-7.30pm Tue-Sat 🚌 🚋 🚋 to Porta Nuova

Galleria Alberto Peola (5, D1)
Established in the late 1980s, this gallery devotes itself to emerging and contemporary artists and is an excellent space to view the works of Turin-based photographers such

as Botto e Bruno, Monica Carocci and Chiara Pirito.
☎ 011 812 44 60
🖥 www.albertopeola.com ✉ Via della Rocca 29 € free ⏱ 3.30-7.30pm Mon-Sat 🚌 🚋 to Piazza Vittorio Veneto

Gas Art Gallery (4, A5)
ith its roots in advertising, this is a very slick space with a sterling roll call of modern artists staging regular exhibitions by such leading local lights as Laura Ambrosi, Piero Gilardi and Ugo Nespoli, plus foreign artists such as photographer Spencer Tunick. It's close to GAM (see p17).
☎ 011 1970 00 31
🖥 www.gasart.it, Italian only ✉ Corso Vittorio Emanuele II 90 € free ⏱ 3-8pm Tue-Sat 🚌 to Stazione Porta Nuova

Vitamin Arte Contemporanea (3, E7)
This edgy space plays host to works by contemporary artists from Europe and takes part in events such as Artissima. It's a good spot to get up to speed on what's happening art-wise in the city, thanks to its owners Maurizio de Giuli and Marta Goglia.
☎ 011 813 66 00
🖥 www.vitaminart.it ✉ Corso San Maurizio 73b € free ⏱ 4-7.30pm Tue-Sat 🚌 🚋 to Piazza Vittorio Veneto

---

Pierced Piazzetta

Don't forget to look up towards the southwestern end of Piazzetta Corpus Domini, at **Palazzo di Città 19** (4, E2), when you pass through this delightful spot. You'll find that one corner of an 18th-century building here has been pierced, with blue blood seeping from one side (a reference to the building's posh inhabitants), and red blood seeping from the other. It's the work of Corrado Levi and Gruppo Cliostraat, a local group of young artists and architects, and was installed in 1996 as part of Cliostraat's Urban Kisses project.

NOTABLE BUILDINGS & MONUMENTS

Atrium Torino (4, C4)
Nicknamed *'giandujotto'*
due to their chocolate-like
shape, these controversial
twin structures in posh Piazza Solferino contain both
the Torino 2006 Winter
Olympics information office
(Atrium2006) and the
main tourist information
office **(AtriumCittà)** for
the city. The structures are
made of wood, steel and
glass and were designed by
Giorgietto Giugiarro, whose
previous claim to fame was
as a car designer. Another
notable aspect of the building is the world's largest
sofa – a serpentine leather
affair made by Piergiorgio
Robino. Multilingual guided
tours are conducted daily.
☎ 011 516 20 06
🖳 www.atriumtorino.it
✉ Piazza Solferino
€ free 🕑 9.30am-7pm
🚌 to Piazza Solferino
♿ good

Lingotto (6, A4-A5)
This hulking Modernist/
Futurist masterpiece, now a
congress centre/exhibition
hall/shopping mall, was
(until 1982) where FIAT
cars were manufactured.
Constructed between 1912
and 1923 and recently
transformed by architect
Renzo Piano, it features
the distinctive ball of blue
glass *(La Bolla)* sheltering a
conference room at the top
and the Pinacoteca Giovanni
e Mariella Agnelli (see p16).
There's also FIAT's legendary rooftop car testing
track (accessible from the
Pinacoteca), which turned
the building itself into a
perpetual motion machine,
as the production process
started on the lower levels,
spiralled up via a ramp
through the building and
then finished on the roof.
✉ Via Nizza 280
€ admission free

🕑 10am-10pm Tue-Sun,
noon-10pm Mon 🚌 1, 35
🚊 18 ♿ good

**Palazzetto Scaglia di
Verrua (4, D2)**
This 16th-century palazzo
isn't really open to the
public, but you'll catch sight
of some beautiful external
frescoes as you pass along
Via Stampatori, and its two
cortile (courtyards) are open
occasionally.
✉ Via Stampatori 4
€ free 🕑 courtyard
9am-noon Thu Feb-Jun &
Sep-Nov 🚌 🚊 to Piazza
Castello ♿ good

Palazzo Carpano (4, E4)
Designed by Michelangelo
Garove at the end of the 17th
century, with amendments
by Benedetto Alfieri, this
beautiful building houses
the Carpano company's HQ,
and is not open to the public.
Mind you, a polite hello and
'posso?' ('May I?') should see
you able to poke your head
into the wonderful, vine-
covered central courtyard.
✉ Via Maria Vittoria 4
🚌 🚊 to Piazza Castello

Palazzo Chiablese (4, F2)
This striking baroque edifice,
constructed in the 17th
century with 18th-century
alterations by the hand of
Benedetto Alfieri, used to
house the collection of the
Museo Nazionale del Cinema,
which was moved to the
Mole Antonelliana in 2000.
It now houses the Soprain-
tendenza de Belle Arti and is
not open to the public.
✉ Piazza San Giovanni 2
🚌 🚊 to Porta Palazzo

The Italian Job
Film buffs, car nuts and Michael Caine fans will all
feel a soft spot for Turin thanks to the feel-good heist
flick *The Italian Job*, filmed in Turin in the late 1960s.
For a guided tour in a vintage Mini Cooper, check
out www.italianjob-tour.com. Some of the famous
locations include:
- **Chiesa di Gran Madre di Dio** (3, E7, p38) The
  steps leading up to the church were the ones
  Michael Caine famously careered down.
- **Lingotto** (6, A4, p34) The former FIAT factory's
  rooftop car testing/racing track was put to excellent use and still draws sighs from misty-eyed
  carspotters.
- **Via Po** (4, G4) One of Turin's most recognisable
  streets, with over 1km of porticoed stunt driving
  opportunities.

The Atrium Torino stays still; you can find it in Piazza Solferino

Palazzo dal Pozzo della Cisterna (4, F4)

Since 1940 this fine structure has housed the offices of the Provincia di Torino and it's an excellent example of the neo-Renaissance and neo-baroque styles of the late 18th century. In 1867, the palace was the main residence of the Dukes of Aosta, although it was originally owned by the Dal Pozzo family in 1685.

✉ **Via Maria Vittoria 12**
⏱ **9am-12.30pm Sat, only gardens can be visited**
🚃 🚋 **to Piazza Castello**

Palazzo dell'Università (4, G3)

Turin's uni students are a lucky lot – they get to call this impressive Piedmontese baroque edifice their alma mater. Designed by Michelangelo Garove and constructed between 1713 and 1720, it features a courtyard that you can take a peek at, although access is not really possible to other parts of the building unless you're a student or faculty member.

✉ **Via Po 17** ⏱ **varies**
🚃 🚋 **to Via Po**

Palazzo Faletti di Barolo (4, D1)

This beautiful, partially renovated palazzo lies in the heart of the Quadrilatero Romano and was commissioned in 1692. It features a typical 'scissors' staircase, which was placed (unusually for the time) in the centre of the building. The palace interior features plenty of baroque stucco detailing and some suitably lavish rooms, but it is also worth noting that the author Silvio Pellico lived here between 1830 and 1854. Guided tours (Italian only) are available.

☎ **011 436 03 11**
🖥 **www.palazzobarolo .it, Italian only**
✉ **Via delle Orfane 7**
€ **€4.15/2.30** ⏱ **10am-noon & 3-5pm Mon & Wed, 10am-noon Fri**
🚃 🚋 **to Porta Palazzo**

Palazzo Lascaris di Ventimiglia (4, D4)

This building has a lavish internal courtyard, although the building itself houses the Consiglio Regionale del Piemonte (Piedmont Regional Council) and, as such, is not open to the public. The exterior is worth a look however. It was constructed between 1663 and 1665.

✉ **Via Alfieri 19**
🚃 **to Piazza Solferino**

Ponte Vittorio Emanuele I (3, E7)

Chances are you'll cross the River Po via this bridge, which was constructed between 1810 and 1815 and connects mammoth Piazza Vittorio Veneto with Piazza Gran Madre di Dio. It's a great spot to stop and take photos, especially looking upriver toward Ponte Umberto I.

🚃 🚋 **to Piazza Vittorio Veneto**

Porta Palatina (4, E1)

A little northwest of the city's Roman amphitheatre you'll find the red-brick remains of Porta Palatina, the city's northern, Roman-era gate. The gate is situated in an enclosed area, but good views of it can be had from a number of points nearby, and there are plans to pedestrianise

Undercover Turin

Turin is not a bad place to get caught in a sudden downpour without an umbrella. After all, the city has a staggering 18km of porticoed walkways, meaning that if you plan your stroll right, you need never care what the weather brings.

this part of the Quadrilatero Romano, making the area more attractive.
✉ **Via Porta Palatina**
🚌 🚊 **to Porta Palazzo**

Spina Centrale (3, A8)
Three million sq metres of reclaimed land are slowly being turned into a backbone of arty offerings in the middle of the city, the first of which was Torino-based Mario Merz's (1925–2003) *Igloo*, located near the Fondazione Sandretto Re Rebaudengo (p14). Other works by artists such as Per Kirkeby, Jannis Kounellis and Michelangelo Pistoletto will grace the area by the time you read this.
✉ **from Corso Mediterraneo** 🚌 **58, 58/**

Synagogue (5, B1)
If you're in the San Salvario neighbourhood you may well find yourself admiring the Oriental strangeness of Turin's 19th-century synagogue, which was built after it was decided to forget about Antonelli's Mole. The synagogue is adjacent to a small piazza dedicated to the writer Primo Levi.
☎ **011 669 23 87**
✉ **Via San Pio V 12**
🕐 **by appointment**
🚌 🚊 🚊 **to Porta Nuova**

Teatro Carignano (4, F3)
Turin's most beautiful theatre (built in 1711) drips with luxury from another age – it's all blood-red velvet, lashings of gilt detail and sparkling chandeliers. Pay a visit via a guided tour if you want to get really close to the furnishings or pop in for a performance – Teatro Stabile regularly has performances here.
☎ **011 516 94 11, box office** ☎ **011 517 62 46**
🖥 **www.teatrostabile torino.it, Italian only**
✉ **Piazza Carignano 6**
🚌 🚊 **to Piazza Castello**

Villa della Regina (3, F8)
Over the Po and set into a wooded hill, the 17th-century Villa della Regina was chosen by Queen Anne d'Orleans, the wife of Vittorio Amedeo, as her hillside residence. Currently closed for restoration, it's on the Unesco World Heritage List. Renovations are slated for completion in 2005, although a reopening date was not known at the time of writing.
✉ **Strada Santa Margherita 40** 🕐 **closed for renovations** 🚌 **53, 55, 56, 66**

It's not always best to ask locals for directions

PIAZZE

Piazza Carlo Emanuele II (4, G5)

This square was laid out with palaces and churches between 1675 and 1684. Daughters of the aristocracy studied at the convent and **Chiesa di Santa Croce** (1718–30) on the square's southern side, while the brightest of the poor attended the nearby **Collegio delle Province** (1737). Someone filthy rich resided at **Palazzo Coardi di Carpeneto** (1680), a palace at No 17 with an 18th-century stuccoed façade and ornate courtyard. Today it's a fine spot to enjoy a coffee (Societé Lutéce; p71).

🚌 🚋 to Via Po

Piazza Castello (4, F3)

At the heart of the historic centre, Turin's grandest square is the perfect place to start exploring the city. In fact, you could easily spend a day or two investigating the wealth of museums, theatres and cafés lining its porticoed promenades. Essentially baroque, the piazza was laid out from the 14th century to serve as the seat of dynastic power for the House of Savoy. Designed to reflect their ambitions for Turin as one of Europe's great capitals, it was steadily transformed by architects such as Filippo Juvarra (1678–1736) into the magnificent space that survives today.

🚌 🚋 to Piazza Castello

Piazza CLN (4, E5)

This fascist-era eyesore gets its mouthful of a name (Pi-

Emanuele Filiberto horsing around, Piazza San Carlo.

azza Comitato di Liberazione Nazionale) abbreviated to the more manageable Piazza CLN and contains two large fountains that represent the city's famous rivers – the Po and the Dora.

🚌 🚌 🚋 to Porta Nuova

Piazza Palazzo di Città (4, E2)

Laid out in the 18th century by Benedetto Alfieri, this area was the location of the forum in Roman-era Turin. It is graced by a sturdy monument to the Conte Verde and a regular market of organic local produce (see p55). It's something of an administrative hub too, with the Town Hall located on the piazza.

🚌 🚋 to Piazza Castello or Porta Palazzo

Piazza San Carlo (4, E4)

Known as Turin's elegant drawing room, Piazza San Carlo (built from 1637 to 1660) acts as something of an aperitif for the banquet that is Piazza Castello. In

fact, aperitifs are central to life on the square, with several historic cafés to be found in its characteristic porticoes. When we visited, the piazza was the scene for frenzied construction activity, as builders went about turning it into a pedestrian space in time for the Winter Olympics.

🚌 🚋 to Piazza Castello or Porta Nuova

Piazza Savoia (4, C1)

Dominated by an obelix that commemorates the abolition of the ecclesiastical court in 1850, Piazza Savoia features some sculptural emblems representative of the city – *grissini* (breadsticks) and Barbera wine! There a couple of good places to come for a drink at night here – see p90.

🚌 🚋 to Porta Palazzo

Piazza Statuto (3, C5)

The black heart of Turin is believed to be located in Piazza Statuto, and anyone who's spent enough time

Glassed In

Turin has three glass-covered galleries, each of them worth seeking out. The most famous of the trio is **Galleria Subalpina** (Galleria dell'Industria Subalpina; 4, F3), which connects Piazza Castello with Piazza Carlo Alberto and contains a cinema, plus some of the city's most beautiful antique shops. **Galleria San Federico** (4, E4) is a T-shaped structure that runs off Via Roma and contains a few fancy fashion boutiques plus the lovely Art-Deco Lux cinema. Near the raucous Porta Palazzo markets you might stumble upon **Galleria Umberto I** (4, E1), which has a faded grandeur that's quite a contrast to the previous galleries. Instead of luxury shops you'll find working-class shops stocking household goods and a few down-at-heel cafés. Get in quick before the gentrification starts.

waiting for buses around this area may well agree. It's also the site of a diabolically bad monument to those who died digging the Fréjus tunnel. For more about this black heart, see p41.

🚌 🚃 🚋 to Porta Susa or 🚌 to Piazza Statuto

Piazzetta Andrea Viglongo (4, C3)

This small piazza looks run-of-the-mill at first glance but a closer inspection reveals half a dozen wave-shaped steel ledges affixed to the side of one its buildings. Even closer inspection reveals that vari-

ous foreign words (Spanish, French, German, Italian and English) meaning 'more' are spelt backwards on the ledges, and the shadows cast by the words onto the wall reveal them during daylight. It's the work of artist Nancy Dwyer.

🚌 🚋 to Piazza Castello

CHURCHES & CATHEDRALS

Chiesa del Corpus Domini (4, E2)

This 17th-century church was designed by Ascanio Vitozzi and sits in the small *piazzetta* that seems to extend from Piazza Palazzo di Città. Rumour has it that in the mid-15th century a soldier attempted to sell a stolen chalice on this spot, and that a host fell from his bag (or his pocket) and rose up into the sky. You can see the story of this miracle inside the church itself.

☎ 011 436 60 25
✉ Piazzetta Corpus Domini € free ⏱ 7.30-11.30am & 3-6pm
🚌 🚋 to Piazza Castello

Chiesa della Gran Madre di Dio (3, E7)

This imposing church,

with its heavy dome and staircase was built between 1818 and 1831 to commemorate the return of Vittorio Emanuele I from exile and is definitely worth a look. Some mystics would have you believe that the Holy Grail lies buried under the church (so that's where it got to!), mostly due to a sculpture holding a chalice that seems to be looking seriously at a certain spot. At noon on 24 June the sun hits the top front of the building fair and square.

☎ 011 819 35 72
✉ Piazza Gran Madre di Dio 4 € free
⏱ 7.30am-noon & 4-7pm 🚌 🚋 to Piazza Vittorio Veneto

Chiesa di San Filippo Neri (4, F4)

The southern flank of Piazza Carignano is blessed by this 1714 church designed by Filippo Juvarra. It's a large, single-aisled church with an impressively simple barrel-vaulted ceiling that seems in marked contrast to the imposing neoclassical façade that was designed by Carlo Giuseppe Talucchi. Light floods the structure via its circular windows placed in the vault and the acoustics are said to be excellent, making this a rather charming spot for occasional music recitals.

☎ 011 54 11 36 ✉ Via Maria Vittorio 5 € free
⏱ 8am-noon & 4.30-7pm Mon-Sat, 10am-noon Sun
🚌 🚋 to Piazza Castello

Chiesa di San Lorenzo (4, F2)

Tucked away in the north-western corner of Piazza Castello is this externally unprepossessing 17th-century church with a richly complex octagonal interior designed by Guarino Guarini. Its dome, with intercepting arches, forms another octagonal shape and the elaborate decorations of stucco garlands and angels are stunning. There's also a large photocopy of the Shroud of Turin on the premises, and far less crowds viewing it here than the one at the *duomo*.

☎ 011 436 15 27
✉ Piazza Castello
€ free ✆ 7.30am-noon & 4-7.30pm Mon-Sat, 9am-1pm, 4-7.30pm & 8.30-10pm Sun 🚌 🚋 to Piazza Castello

Chiesa di Santa Croce (4, G5)

This proud church, which stands on Piazza Carlina (as Piazza Carlo Emanuele II is known), was designed by Juvarra and built by the Augustinians in the latter half of the 19th century. Inside there's a notable work by Beaumont of the *Deposition*.

☎ 011 812 67 03
✉ Piazza Carlo Emanuele

A feathered friend of the Chiesa di San Filippo Neri

II ✆ closed for renovation 🚌 🚋 to Piazza Castello

Chiese di San Carlo e di Santa Cristina (4, E4)

These twin baroque churches grace the bottom end of Piazza San Carlo (where it meets unattractive Piazza CLN). Construction on San Carlo and Santa Cristina began in 1619, but the buildings were not finished until some time later. The façade of Santa Cristina is the work of none other than Filippo Juvarra.

☎ 011 53 92 81
✉ Piazza CLN 231 bis
€ free ✆ San Carlo

7am-noon & 4-7pm Mon-Fri, 9am-1pm Sat & Sun, Santa Cristina not open to public 🚌 🚋 🚋 to Porta Nuova

Santuario di Maria Consolatrice (La Consolata) (3, C5)

It's not the city's *duomo*, but it's certainly the citizens' favourite church in Turin, and you can always find someone in this baroque sanctuary. There has been a place of worship on this site since the 11th century (indeed, the bell tower is a remnant from this time), although the current structure displays the influence of a number of architects and architectural styles. One of the most fascinating aspects is the wall of pictures giving thanks to Mary for assistance during various disasters and illnesses.

☎ 011 436 32 35
✉ Piazza della Consolata
€ free ✆ 24hr
🚌 52, 60

Torino Card

Serious sightseers can invest €15/17 (48/72 hours) in a Torino Card, sold by tourist offices and covering admission to 120 monuments and museums in and around Turin. It also provides discounts of 50% on selected theatre and concert tickets, bicycle hire, guided tours and so on, plus you'll travel for free on public transport in the city (see also p117).

PARKS & GARDENS

Giardini Reale (4, G2)
These lovely gardens are a surprisingly untouristed spot, given their central location and great beauty. They were designed in 1697 by Andrè le Nôtre, who also created the gardens of Versailles. This a wonderful spot to escape the hustle and bustle of nearby Piazza Castello.
✉ **Viale Luzio**
€ **free** ☺ **9am-1hr before sunset** 🚌 🚊 **to Piazza Castello**

Orto Botanico (5, C3)
Turin's Botanic Gardens are much admired and make for a pleasant getaway as you stroll southwest along the River Po. The gardens date from 1729 and are tended by green-thumbed university professors, which means you'll find some interesting themes among the 4000-strong selection of flora. Access for the visually impaired is very good.
☎ **011 661 24 47**
🖥 **www.bioveg.unito .it** ✉ **Via Mattioli 25**
€ **€3/1.50** ☺ **9am-1pm & 3-7pm Sat & Sun Apr-Sep, by appointment only other times** 🚌 🚊 🚇 **to Porta Nuova** ♿ **good**

Parco del Valentino (5, C2)
This carefully designed French-style park opened in 1856 and is one of the most celebrated parks in Italy – particularly by joggers, cyclists and smooching young romancers, who all appreciate its 550,000 sq metres of verdant space. It's a delightful, family-friendly spot during the day and popular during the summer as a nightlife zone, as it has some delightful outdoor cafés and bars. Don't forget to visit the Fontana dei Mesi, designed by Carlo Ceppi in 1898 which represents the months of the year. At night, it's best to avoid the park if you're solo.
✉ **Corso Vittorio Emanuele II** € **free**
☺ **24hr** 🚌 🚊 🚇 **to Porta Nuova**

Parco Naturale Collina Torinese (2, E2)
This green retreat is only a short distance from the city but seems miles away thanks to its tranquillity and open spaces. You can find woods, meadows, vineyards, birds and critters and enjoy some charming views of the surrounding area. If you'd like to explore the park by bicycle, the info office rents out bikes, and night-time hikes are also arranged.
☎ **011 890 36 67**
🖥 **www.parks.it/parco .collina.torinese/**
✉ **Stazione Tranvia, Strada Funicolare 55**
€ **free** ☺ **office 9.30am-noon & 2-5pm** 🚋 **Tranvia Superga**

Parco del Valentino, popular by day and night – honestly

A City of Two Hearts

Turin is a city of magic. Home to the Holy Shroud and, according to legend, of the Holy Grail, it's a sacred town with a diabolical core. Situated on the 45th parallel, it forms one of the three apexes of the so-called white magic triangle with Lyon and Prague and of the black magic triangle with London and San Francisco.

Mysterious and ancient lines of positive and negative energy converge on the city, as do two rivers, the Po and the Dora. The Po is said to represent the sun and the masculine while the Dora symbolises the moon and the feminine. Together they form a protective ring of water around the city.

The black heart of Turin is **Piazza Statuto** (3, C5). The Romans believed it to be cursed, as its position was unfavourable for sunset, which symbolised the convergence of good and evil. More prosaically, Piazza Statuto was the site of the city scaffold where thousands met their fate before passing directly through the Gates of Hell. On the other side of the divide, legend places the Gates of Infinity in **Piazza Solferino** (4, C4).

Piazza Castello is the centre of the white magic map. Believers cite as reasons for the purity of this area the vicinity of the Holy Shroud in the Duomo di San Giovanni Battista, the positive energies emanating from the Museo Egizio and the golden auspices of the cave under Palazzo Madama, where the Savoys used to have the master alchemists of the day practise their mysterious arts.

QUIRKY TURIN

Antica Erboristeria della Consolata (3, C5)

This beautiful old herbalist's is located in Turin's most charming piazza and seems pretty much unchanged from the day it opened its doors. It's still a thriving business, so feel free to have any ailment sorted out with the wonderful range of natural products available, but make sure you keep an eye on the Harry Potter-style surrounds while you do so.
☎ 011 436 67 10
✉ Piazza Consolata 5
€ free ⏱ 8.30am-12.30pm & 3-7.30pm Tue-Sat, 3-7.30pm Mon
🚌 🚊 to Porta Palazzo

Borgo Medievale (3, D9)

At first sight, this place may have you thinking that there are more remnants of medieval Turin than you'd been led to believe, but a closer inspection reveals that not one skerrick of this place is authentic. It's a bizarre Disney-style simulacrum of a medieval settlement, and strangely popular with locals. The castle and its surrounds were built for the Italian General Exhibition of 1884. Not a bad place to take the kids.
✉ Viale Virgilio 107
€ castle €3/2, village free ⏱ 9am-7pm Oct-Mar, 9am-8pm Apr-Sep
🚊 9, 16

Hammam Al Bab (3, D5)

More than just a *hammam* (Turkish-style bathhouse), this delightful place also has Al Andalus (p72),

a great Middle-Eastern restaurant on the premises, as well as a cultural centre. What draws crowds though are various soothing treatments for the body, such as massages and scrubs (which cost extra and require bookings). You'll find this oasis of relaxation in the multicultural streets near the rowdy Porta Palazzo markets (p12).
☎ 011 521 64 96
🖳 www.hamam -torino.it, Italian only
✉ Via Fiochetto 15
€ 10-12/6 ⏱ Women Tue, Thu & Sat, Men Wed, Fri & Sun 🚌 🚊 to Porta Palazzo

Via Roma (4, E4)

What's so quirky about a street crammed with stores selling luxury goods and

other wares? Try and find another business…that's right, there's a kilometre-long stretch of nothing but retail on Via Roma, and even the inhabitants of the offices and apartments above ground level will generally have to enter their buildings via side-street entrances.
🖥 www.torino-viaroma.com € free 🕒 24hr 🚇 🚇 🚇 to Porta Nuova or Piazza Castello

If you don't find what you want, just keep walking

TURIN FOR CHILDREN

Bambini (children) are welcomed with open arms in Italy, although Turin is more subdued on this front than some other places. Nappy-changing facilities, high chairs and cots are far from commonplace and children are generally not taken to the more expensive restaurants. One excellent development was the January 2005 Italy-wide law that prohibited smoking in bars, restaurants and other public places, meaning that if you are dining out with your littlies, they need not be breathing second-hand smoke.

Pharmacies sell baby formula, sterilising solutions and nappies. Nappies are also sold at supermarkets, as is fresh milk.

Children under three enter museums and other sights for free; those aged three to 12 pay half-price. The same applies to public transport. Look for the 🚼 listed with individual reviews in the Eating, Entertainment and Sleeping chapters for more kid-friendly options. For more information, see Lonely Planet's *Travel with Children* or the websites www.travelwithyourkids.com and www.familytravelnetwork.com.

Burattini al Borgo
The muggy months of July to September see regular puppet shows for all the family at the Piazza del Melograno in Borgo Medievale (3, D9; p41). Shows are performed by the established and respected Marionette Grilli company.
☎ 011 819 58 30
🖥 www.marionet tegrilli.com, Italian only ✉ Piazza del Melograno, Borgo Medievale 🕒 Jul-Sep 🚇 9, 16

Experimenta (3, F7)
Attracting children to the world of science is what Experimenta is all about. The city's former zoo becomes an interactive science fair with lots of very interesting and amusing

Babysitters
The City of Turin publishes a list of Turin-based babysitters who all get the city's stamp of approval; follow the 'English Version/Turin for Children/Useful Numbers' link at www.comune.torino.it.

exhibits and demonstrations on offer.

☎ 011 432 44 14
🖳 www.experimenta
.to.it ✉ Parco Michelotti, Corso Casale 15
€ €6.50/4 ⏱ 4pm-midnight Tue-Fri, 3pm-midnight Sat, 10am-8pm Sun Jun–mid-Sep 🚌 3

Museo della Marionetta (4, D4)

Children will enjoy the laughs to be had at this Marionette Museum, which houses a vast collection of period puppets, costumes and props, as well as a puppet theatre, the Teatro Gianduja. Those with a puppet phobia (and there are plenty of us) had better steer clear.

☎ 011 53 03 28 🖳 mus
eomarionettelupi@tin
.it ✉ Via Santa Teresa
5 € €2.60 ⏱ 9.30am-
1pm & 2.30-5.30pm

Mon-Fri, by appointment
🚌 🚋 to Piazza Castello
♿ limited

Teatroregio (4, G3)

Get your kids started on high culture with the **Opera...ndo con Mamma e Papà** series for children. Sessions last for three hours and include tours, games, opera highlights, demonstrations and a lot of laughs. Even if your child doesn't speak Italian, there's enough fun to be had here to translate into enjoyment.

☎ 011 881 52 09
🖳 www.teatroregio
.torino.it, Italian only
✉ Piazza Castello 215
€ adult/concession
€5/4, child 6-10 free
⏱ check with box office
for times 🚌 🚋 to
Piazza Castello
♿ good

Short films for short attention spans at the Museo Nazionale del Cinema

Out & About

WALKING TOURS
Going for Baroque

You can't do all of Turin's baroque jewels in a day, but you can do the big ones. Starting from Piazza Castello, where you'll find the **Palazzo Reale** (**1**; p19) and the **Chiesa di San Lorenzo** (**2**; p39), take Via Palazzo di Città until Via XX Settembre. Go right and you'll find the Duomo di San Giovanni and the **Cappella della Santa Sindone** (**3**; p22). Returning to the square, head for **Palazzo Madama** (**4**; p20) and, continuing down Via Po, **Palazzo dell'Università** (**5**; p35). From here Via Bogino heads southwards past **Palazzo Granieri** (**6**; Via Bogino 9) to Via Maria Vittoria. Go left at Via Maria Vittoria for Piazza Carlo Emanuele II and its three baroque beauties: **Palazzo Coardi di Carpeneto** (**7**), the **Collegio delle Province** (**8**) and the **Chiesa di Santa Croce** (**9**). Via Accademia Albertina leads to Via Giovanni Giolitti, which you turn right into and head down until Piazza San Carlo. Here the **Chiesa di Santa Cristina** (**10**; p39) will sustain you for the last leg down Via Accademia della Scienze. Before you plunge down this imposing road, take a peek at **Chiesa di San Filippo Neri** (**11**; p38), before passing the **Accademia delle Scienze** (**12**; p13) on your left, and finally fabulous **Palazzo Carignano** (**13**; p25) further down on your right.

distance 2.6km
duration 3.5hr
▶ **start** 🚋 🚌 to Piazza Castello
● **end** 🚋 🚌 from Piazza Carignano

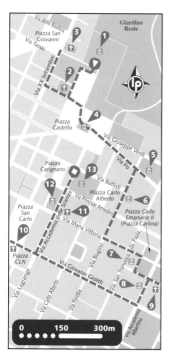

Got a window for coffee? Piazza San Carlo

The Devil's in the Details

Some of Turin's spookier and over-looked details are brought to light in this stroll. Start at the north of **Piazza Solferino** (**1**), where the **Fontana Angelica** (**2**), in front of Atrium Torino, represents the four seasons and is embellished with a whole lot of Masonic imagery and symbolism. Freemasonry is a re-putedly shadowy political force in Italian politics, so Masonic details in this area are often seen as signs of something a little sinister. Leg-end also places the Gates of Infinity at this site (see p41). From here, walk to **No 7** (**3**), where a strik-ingly carved door exhibits more Masonic signifiers. At Via Alfieri

Get beside Atrium Torino, Piazza Solferino

15, you'll find **Palazzo Lascaris di Ventimiglia** (**4**; p35), which sports extraordinary stone carvings – note that the 'nice' ones are all the same, while the 'nasty' ones are vastly different to each other. On the corner of Via XX Settembre and Via Alfieri` you'll see the door nicknamed **la porta del diau** (**5**, local dialect for 'the devil's door'). Typically Piedmon-tese in style, it features a gruesome doorknocker that depicts two snakes coming out of the devil's mouth and numerous flowers and *putti* (cherub's heads). The building itself has a

distance 350m
duration 1hr
▶ **start** 🚌 to Piazza Solferino
● **end** 🚌 🚆 from Via XX Settembre

reputation for murderous goings on in the past and was where tarot cards where sold in the 18th cen-tury. It's now a bank, as are many of the diabolically decorated build-ings in and around this quarter.

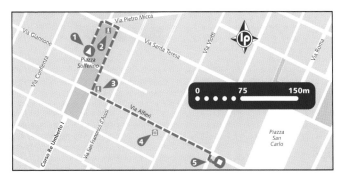

Po-faced

Though you start in the centre of town, you'll soon find yourself in the fresh air with this walk. Commence strolling from the top of porticoed **Via Po** (**1**), with its **Palazzo dell'Università** (**2**; p35), before you reach magnificent **Piazza Vittorio Veneto** (**3**) – one of Europe's grandest squares. Cross **Ponte Vittorio Emanuele I** (**4**; p35) and the River Po (don't miss the wonderful views down the river) to get a closer look at the monumental

distance 2.5km
duration 4hr
▶ start 🚍 🚋 9, 16 to Via Po
● end 🚃 Borgo Medievale

Bigger than most; Gran Madre di Dio

Chiesa della Gran Madre di Dio (**5**; p38). Cross back to the other side of the river and then walk along Via Murazzi del Po, where the **Murazzi** (**6**; p83) clubs and bars line the riverfront. If it's summer, pop into one of the daytime openers for an alfresco drink or two. From **Imbarco Murazzi** (**7**; p51) take a boat a short way upstream to **Parco del Valentino** (**8**; p40) and the **Borgo Medievale** (**9**; p41). Take as much time as you like to walk along the park's paths and soak up the wonderful greenery and marvel at the extraordinary sense of tranquillity this close to the city centre.

Eat, Drink & Be Merry

You don't have to ingest or imbibe something at every spot on this tour in fact we would recommend against it – but be sure to make a point of noting where these places are for future reference. When it comes to Turin's eating scene, the mother lode can be found at the **Porta Palazzo Market** (**1**; p12). From here, walk east to Piazza Emanuele Filiberto, then left down Via delle Orfane before turning right into Piazza della Consolata and enjoying a quintessentially Turinese *bicerin* at **Al Bicerin** (**2**; p84). From here, head back down Via delle Orfane to Via Giuseppe Garibaldi, Europe's 'longest pedestrian mall', and on to Piazza Castello, where tiny **Caffè Mulassano** (**3**; p86) shines. Duck into the gorgeous **Galleria Subalpina** (**4**; p41) to peer into the windows of **Baratti & Milano** (**5**; p85), then exit at the southern end of the galleria and head right

at Via Battisti, arriving in Piazza Carignano and the lavish truffle-serving lunch spot of Cavour, **Ristorante del Cambio** (**6**; p70) and ice-cream purveyor extraordinaire **Pepino** (**7**; p74). From the piazza, take Via Roma south to Piazza San Carlo, the city's elegant 'drawing room', where you can pull up a chair at the historic **Caffè San Carlo** (**8**; p86) or **Caffè Torino** (**9**; p86) before a visit to marvellous master confectioner **Stratta** (**10**; p62) for gifts good enough to keep to yourself – for later, of course.

distance 1.1km
duration 2hr (4hr with lunch)
▶ **start** 🚋 🚎 🚌 to Porta Palazzo
● **end** 🚋 🚎 🚌 from Via Lagrange

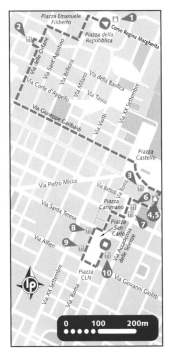

Pepino, Turin's oldest ice cream parlour

DAY TRIPS
Asti   (2, B2)

The best place in Italy for a bottle of bubbly, Asti is the capital of the sparkling-wine industry. A monument to Asti's 13th-century hey-day, the 44m-tall **Torre Troyana o dell'Orologio** (☎ 0141 39 94 60; Piazza Medici; admission free; ☻ 10am-1pm & 4-7pm Apr-Sep, 10am-1pm & 3-6pm Sat & Sun Oct) towers over Piazza Medici. You can scale the 199 steps to a 37m-high viewing platform.

Gracing Piazza San Secondo, the Romanesque-Gothic **Chiesa Collegiata di San Secondo** (☎ 0141 53 00 66; Piazza San Secondo; ☻ 10.45am-noon & 3.30-5.30pm Mon-Sat, 3.30-5.30pm Sun) houses the bones of the city's patron saint; legend has it that Secondo was martyred and buried here in AD 119. Adjoining the church is the **Palazzo Municipale**, a splendid 18th-century office building that is not open to the public.

Further afield lies Asti's red-brick **cattedrale** (☎ 0141 59 29 24; Piazza Cattedrale; ☻ 8.30am-noon, 3.30-5.30pm). Dating from the 8th century, it sports three beautiful stained-glass windows.

> **INFORMATION**
> *50km southeast of Turin*
> - 🚆 30-55 minutes
> - 🚍 A10 or SS10 from Turin
> - ℹ tourist office (☎ 0141 53 03 57; www.terredasti.it, in Italian; Piazza Alfieri 29; ☻ 9am-1pm & 2.30-6.30pm Mon-Sat, 9am-1pm Sun)
> - 🍴 Gener Neuve (☎ 0141 55 72 70, Lungo Tarno 4 – 2km south of Piazza Campo del Palio; set menu €60, reservations advised); 3 Bicchieri (☎ 0141 32 41 37; Piazza Statuto 37)

Local Reputation

Within Piedmont, people from Asti are considered the most exuberant. Always armed with a glass of wine and slice of salami in hand, they welcome outsiders and bear a happy-go-lucky attitude towards life. Cheers to that!

A likely contributer to Asti's exuberance

September's flurry of festivals offers ample wine-tasting opportunities: the 10-day **Douja d'Or** (a *douja* being a terracotta wine jug unique to Asti) is followed by the one-day **Delle Sagre** food festival on the second Sunday of the month (a mind-blowing 500,000 people sat down to eat on Piazza Campo del Palio in 2002).

The **Palio**, held in the third weekend in September, sees horses race around Piazza Alfieri. The first mention of horse racing in Asti dates to 1275. On the third Sunday of September, 21 costumed jockeys, from each of the town's historic quarters, gallop bareback around the course set up in Piazza Alfieri.

Alba (2, B3)

Alba's characteristic red-brick towers rise above cobbled squares and make a fine backdrop to its pretty porticoed streets. Its town centre is compact and easy to explore, with the main strip, Via Vittorio Emanuele II, connecting the two central squares, Piazza Savona and Piazza Risorgimento. From Piazza Risorgimento head northwest along Via Cavour for Piazza Medford. Alba is surrounded by some of Piedmont's most attractive and productive countryside. Extending south and east of town, the green hills of the Langhe are famous for their majestic red wines.

> **Truffle Mania**
> A gastronomic mecca in the heart of red-wine country, Alba is famed throughout Italy for its highly sought-after white truffles. The town's popular white truffle fair takes place in October.

Alba's most photographed landmarks are its red-brick **Torre Medioevale** (medieval towers), which loom over Piazza Risorgimento. Originally built as monuments to the wealth and taste of the town's 14th- and 15th-century nobility, only about 20 remain today. The best-preserved are still impressive, particularly when lit up at night. Unfortunately it is not possible to climb any of them.

The **Cattedrale di San Lorenzo** has undergone numerous restorations over many years. It dates back to the early 12th century and is much altered from its original Gothic appearance – its last facelift took place in 2004.

Dedicated museum-goers can investigate Alba's Roman and prehistoric past at the **Museo Civico Federico Eusebio** (☎ 0173 29 24 73; Via Paruzza 1; €4/2.50; 🕙 4-7pm Mon-Fri, 9.30am-12.30pm & 4-7pm Sat & Sun), which houses a modest collection of prehistoric and Roman artefacts as well as a selection of minerals and fossilised bugs.

> **INFORMATION**
> *60km south of Turin*
> - 🚆 50 minutes
> - 🚌 A6 from Turin, then SS231 to Alba
> - ℹ️ main tourist office (☎ 0173 3 58 33; www.langheroero.it; Piazza Medford 3; 🕙 9am-12.30pm & 2.30-6.30pm Mon-Fri, 9am-12.30pm Sat)
> - 🍴 L'Osteria del Teatro (☎ 0173 36 46 03; Via Generale Govone 7; 🕙 Tue-Thu)

Comes up all right after a spit and polish...

Pinerolo (2, A2)

Pinerolo is a pleasant town with a lovely *centro storico* (historic centre) that makes a good half-day trip from Turin or a base for exploring the nearby valleys of Val Chisone.

The **Museo Nazionale dell'Arma di Cavalleria** (☎ 0121 37 63 44; Viale Giolitti 5; admission free; 9-11.30am & 2-4pm Tue-Thu, 9-11.30am Sat & Sun) is spread over three floors and displays uniforms, flags, regimental paraphernalia and a comprehensive collection of weapons.

Almost directly behind this is the **Civico Museo Etnografico e Museo del Legno** (Municipal Museum of Local Customs and Traditions and Museum of Wood; ☎ 0121 79 43 82; Via Brignone 3; admission free; 10.30am-noon & 3.30-6pm), which tells the story of life in Val Chisone, Val Pellice and Val Germanasca.

In the *centro storico* the 10th-century **Duomo di San Donato** (Piazza San Donato; admission free; 7am-noon & 2.30-7pm) is certainly worth a look while, up the hill, the Gothic **Chiesa di San Maurizio** (Piazzale San Maurizio; admission free; 7am-noon & 2.30-7pm) displays a peculiar, one-handed clock.

INFORMATION
40km southwest of Turin
- 🚆 1 hour, 20 daily
- 🚌 SS23 from Turin
- ℹ️ tourist office (☎ 0121 79 40 03; www.montagnedoc.it; Viale Giolitti 7; 9am-12.30pm & 3-6pm Mon-Fri, 10am-1pm & 2-5pm Sat & Sun)
- ✘ Taverna degli Acaja (☎ 0121 79 47 27; Corso Torino 106; closed Sun & lunch Mon)

Bardonecchia (2, A2)

At the head of the Valle di Susa, Bardonecchia is the last stop in Italy before the Fréjus tunnel takes you through to France. Situated in a massive wooded amphitheatre, it is divided into two parts: the modern Borgonuovo (new town) and the atmospheric Borgovecchio (old town).

A favourite of Turin's weekend skiers and an excellent family destination, it's also a relaxed summer resort where visitors come to enjoy the lush green hills. Bardonecchia's main strip is fashionable Via Medail, which heads uphill from near the train station to the Borgovecchio. For ski-lifts head down Viale delle Vittoria.

Very popular in this area are **skiing, snowboarding** and **cross-country**, with well-marked courses (10km for cross-country) and runs (110km for downhill) at altitude and on the valley floor.

INFORMATION
90km west of Turin
- 🚆 1½ hours, 6 daily
- 🚌 A32 from Turin
- ℹ️ tourist office (☎ 0122 9 90 32; www.montagnedoc.it; Viale della Vittoria 4; 9am-12.30pm & 2.30-7pm Mon-Sat)
- ✘ Ristorante Biovey (☎ 0122 99 92 15; Via Generale Cantore 2; Wed-Mon)

ORGANISED TOURS

Discover Olympic Turin (4, C4) See how the city's coping with a massive construction boom and a concurrent case of Olympic fever on this guided tour that visits the 'building yards'. You'll need to be over 12 years of age for this one.
☎ 011 53 51 81
💻 www.turismotorino.com ✉ departs from Atrium 2006, Piazza Solferino € per person €5 🕑 2.30pm Fri

FIAT Mirafiori is the massive (3 million sq metre) FIAT factory complex south of the city centre, said to be the world's largest car factory. No longer keeping 60,000 workers busy (it's about 15,000 now) and facing an uncertain future, now might be the time to see this enormous 20th-century feat of industrial prowess in action. For guided tours (English can be arranged), contact the company directly, and in advance. Get to Mirafiori by either tram No 4 or in a taxi.
☎ 06 003 42 69
✉ Corso Giovanni Agnelli 200 € free 🕑 on request

Ristocolor This brightly painted tram cruises past many of the city's most notable sights and feeds you while you're at it, provided you're in a group (the tram can take up to 32 people). Tours generally depart from Piazza Carlina and the website can tell you when the next trip is.
☎ 011 517 58 86
💻 www.comune.torino it/gtt/turismo/tramrist .shtml ✉ varies € €40 🕑 8.30pm 🚷 limited

Navigazione sul Po (5, E1) Local transport company GTT organises three boat trips that ply the River Po. The 15-minute short trip to the Borgo Medievale in Parco del Valentino departs from Imbarco Murazzi and

---

Guided by Voices

If you really want to make the city come alive on a tour, then a personal itinerary planned for you by an experienced guide might be the way to go. Two excellent English-speaking guides that we can personally recommend are **Pierfranco Viano** (☎ 349 847 73 46) and **Emanuela Moroni** (☎ 347 258 43 05). Both are able to tailor city and local area excursions to your needs, on a number of themes and for individuals and groups.

More happy customers

affords lovely views of the city. They also travel as far as Moncalieri. You can buy tickets on board.
☎ 011 74 48 92
💻 www.comune.torino.it/gtt/turismo/navigazione.shtml ✉ Murazzi del Po 65 € adult return up to €5.20 🕑 6 trips daily mid-Jun–Sep, 6 trips Sat & Sun May–mid-Jun, 3 trips Sun & hols Oct-Apr

Turismo Bus Torino (4, C4) With 14 stops around the city's major sites, this hop-on/hop-off tourist bus covers the bases and offers hourly departures, so you can pay closer attention to certain attractions. Commentary is provided, and you can arrange for English-language explanations. Buy tickets on board or at any Turismo Torino info point. It's free with the Torino card (see p117).
☎ 011 53 51 81
💻 www.turismotorino.org ✉ departs from

Piazza Solferino € 1-day ticket €5/3 🕑 10am-6pm daily Jul-Sep & late-Dec–early Jan, weekends & hols rest of year

Torino Magica (3, B5) There are two fascinating Torino Magica tours on offer, with commentary (English available on request) lasting 2½ hours. You'll get to explore the black- and white-magic points of the city, and never look at the city in quite the same way again. Reservations essential.
☎ 011 668 05 80
💻 www.somewhere.it ✉ begins from Piazza Statuto € per person €20 🕑 9pm Tue, Thu & Sat

Torino Multiculti (4, J5) Turin is a multicultural town, with inhabitants from eastern Europe, Asia, the Middle East and Africa enlivening many of the city's traditional quarters. This

three-hour tour takes in various religious buildings, such as the mosque and Romanian Orthodox church. Reservations essential, and English-language tours can be arranged.
☎ 011 668 05 80
💻 www.somewhere.it ✉ begins from Piazza Vittorio Veneto
€ per person €23
🕑 8.30pm Tue

Torino Sotterranea (4, J5) Don't even think about this one if you're claustrophobic! A three-hour exploration of the city's underbelly sees you wandering along various bomb shelters and secret tunnels built by the Savoys. Reservations essential, and English language guides available. Wear sensible shoes.
☎ 011 668 0580
💻 www.somewhere.it ✉ begins from Piazza Vittorio Veneto
€ per person €25
🕑 8.30pm Wed & Fri

Hop-on/hop-off, Turismo Bus

Shopping

This is Italy – shopping is in the blood, and at times, it may well resemble a blood sport. Turin's shopping scene is every bit as lively and enjoyable as other big Italian cities such as Milan and Rome, and has some particularly delightful speciality stores (antiques, books and chocolate seem to be an obsession), along with the usual array of beautifully presented fashion and homewares stores.

Opening hours in Turin are generally from about 9.30am to 12.30pm and then 3.30pm to 7.30pm from Tuesday to Saturday, with stores opening for the afternoon session on Monday but not at all on Sunday except in December. Many fashion shops close for August, when Italians take their holidays. Sales are held in July and January. Non-EU citizens are entitled to a VAT refund if you spend over €175.50 in stores displaying the 'Tax Free for Tourists' sign. Credit cards will be accepted at most stores, and businesses that deal with collectors and international customers (such as art and antique stores) will be able to arrange postage and shipping.

For details of transport routes listed in this chapter, see p114.

Shopping Strips

Turin's most prestigious shopping street is **Via Roma** (p41) which, on Saturday and Sunday afternoons, throngs with weekend strollers parading beneath its porticoes and peering at its expensive window displays. Unlike most other shops in Turin, these boutiques open from 3pm to 7pm on Sunday. Designer stores also stud parallel **Via Lagrange**.

The elegance of another age is captured in the glass-topped malls of **Galleria Subalpina** (p38), linking Piazza Castello with Via Battisti, and **Galleria San Frederico**, which runs in a T-shape between Via Roma, Via Bertola and Via Santa Teresa. Beautiful art, antiques and bookshops linger in these covered shopping malls.

Porticoed **Via Po**, with its pavement cafés and alternative fashion shops, attracts a younger shopping crowd. In Turin's medieval quarter **Via Mercanti**, with its traditional bookbinders and candlestick makers, is the street to stroll for handmade crafts and unusual souvenirs. **Via Maria Vittoria** is lined with baroque *palazzi* and stunning antique stores of the 'ring the bell' variety. **Via Sant'Agostino** and around holds edgy fashion shops and retro boutiques, while **Via Giuseppe Garibaldi** is a long pedestrianised strip crammed with good-value mainstream fashion shops.

DEPARTMENT STORES & SHOPPING CENTRES

8 Gallery
Despite the predominance of small, family-run shops and designer boutiques, Turin has not been spared the shopping centre. This enormous one, housed in the old FIAT Lingotto factory (6, B4) gets packed on weekends with Turinese looking for everything under the one roof – from shops to a games room to an art gallery to a cinema complex. There's also an enormous supermarket on the premises.
☎ 011 67 32 27
🖥 www.8gallery.it, In Italian ✉ Via Nizza 262 ⏲ 2-10pm Mon, 10am-10pm Tue-Sun
🚌 1, 35 🚋 18 P

Lagrange 15 (4, E5)
Spread over several floors, this is a rather dispirited example of a shopping centre, with numerous tacky retail outlets and an unfortunate display of caged lizards. Still, La Rinascente, the Italian department store, is on the premises, and it's a very handy spot to stock up on fashion basics, such as underwear, umbrellas and cosmetics.
☎ 011 517 00 75
✉ Via Lagrange 15
⏲ 1-8.30pm Mon, 9.30am-8.30pm Tue-Fri, 9.30am-9pm Sat 🚌 🚋 to Porta Nuova

Upim (4, E5)
Just to prove that Via Roma is not completely devoted to the top end of shopping, Upim squats on the corner with Via Cavour and combines good-quality, low-priced fashion with homewares and cosmetic basics in a rather swanky, modern setting. The sort of place where you can observe society ladies stock up on all sorts of goodies whilst pretending not to notice each other.
☎ 011 54 49 57
✉ Via Roma 305
⏲ 1-8pm Mon, 9.30am-8pm Tue-Sat
🚌 🚊 🚋 to Porta Nuova

Dusk is rarely a barrier when it comes to clothes shopping in Turin

MARKETS

A small selection of some of Turin's most notable markets:

Il Balôn (3, D5)

A weekly antique market that draws the curious and the collectors, where everything old is new again. Come here if you can't make it to Il Gran Balôn.

💻 www.balon.it, In Italian ✉ Via Borgo Dora & around 🕑 8am-6pm Sat 🚌 🚊 to Porta Palazzo

Il Gran Balôn (3, D5)

Antique dealers from around the region and even from France hawk their wares at this busy monthly market, which demands your attention if you're lucky enough to be in town for it. Make sure you score a lunch table at Trattoria Valenza (p77) or San Giors (p75) to round out the experience.

💻 www.balon.it, In Italian ✉ Via Borgo Dora & around 🕑 8am-1pm 2nd

---

In the Market for a Good Book

The first Sunday of every month (except August) sees Piazza Carlo Felice's porticoes play host to a rare and specialist book fair, with plenty of bookworms, collectors and dawdlers sniffing around books both well-thumbed and closely guarded.

Sun of month 🚌 🚊 to Porta Palazzo

Mercatino della Crocetta (3, B8)

Something of an open-air boutique for fashion hunters who don't want to pay top euro. There's some trash and some treasure, but it's certainly worth exploring if the wallet's grim. Good people-watching opportunities too, as this is one of the city's bastions of the discreetly charming bourgeoisie.

✉ Via Marco Polo & Largo Cassini 🕑 8.30am-

1pm Mon-Fri 🚌 12, 58, 58/ 🚊 15, 16

Mercatino delle Erbe (4, E2)

Since medieval times this piazza has hosted a produce market, and it's still a wonderful place to find organic and biodynamic regional goodies, including wines. Sampling is not only allowed, it's encouraged.

✉ Piazza Palazzo di Città 🕑 1st Sun of month Mar-Jun & Sep-Dec 🚌 🚊 to Piazza Castello or Porta Palazzo

It isn't worth eating if you can't find it at Turin's markets

CLOTHING

Annacaffè (4, E3)
Imaginative high-end fashion labels such as Lagerfeld and haughty Italian staples can be found at this swanky Via Roma salon. If you need shoes, bags and jewellery to complete the look, that can be arranged too. Service is helpful and can help you put together a whole look, but this can get a little expensive. ☎ 011 517 15 53 ✉ Via Roma 19 ☉ 3-7pm Mon, 10am-7pm Tue-Sat 🚌 🚃 to Piazza Castello

Autopsie Vestimentaire (4, D1)
This is local designer Alice Capelli's atelier, and inside you'll find imaginative, seemingly unstructured creations that won't break the bank. Each price tag tells you exactly how many hours Alice spent making your garment, and she's more than happy to help you work

out ways to wear it, or to create something for you in other sizes or colours (allow about a week). She also stocks interesting shoes and resin and glass jewellery. ☎ 011 436 06 41 ✉ Via Bonelli 6b ☉ 3-7.30pm Tue-Thu, 3-7.30pm & 10.30pm-12.30am Fri & Sat 🚌 🚃 to Porta Palazzo

Carla G (4, E5)
It's true – Italians do it better. Walk into a shop on your home turf, spy a pair of leopard-print shoes or a tiger-print top and you walk out thinking 'slapper'. Here, you let a friendly, comforting-yet-brisk sales assistant convince you that such things work well with smart trousers and elegant skirts. And you know what? They do in Turin. ☎ 011 557 91 31 ✉ Via Lagrange 7c ☉ 3-7.30pm

Mon, 10am-7.30pm Tue-Thu, Fri, 10am-1pm & 3.30-7.30pm Wed & Sat 🚌 🚃 to Via Lagrange

Diesel (4, E5)
Italians have a way of making arse-mincingly, eye-wincingly tight jeans look like the most stylish thing in the world, and if the denim-clad butts of Turin's youth have got you convinced that you should try this at home, then the Diesel store should be your first port of call. Dozens of styles, plenty of sizes, staff you can trust to tell you when too tight really *is* too tight. Prices start at around €110. ☎ 011 511 90 58 ✉ Via Lagrange 24 ☉ 3.30-7.30pm Mon, 10.30am-7.30pm Tue-Sat 🚌 🚃 to Via Lagrange

Galleria Piás (4, D1)
This arty space shows innovative quirky designers

'Sorry, did you say something?'

at their best, and is low-key enough to let you mooch around with the resident pooch and admire such wacky fashion fare as a skirt made entirely out of silk socks or adorable hand-made bags fashioned from felt.

☎ 011 436 15 79
✉ Via Bonelli 11a
🕓 11am-9pm Tue-Sat
🚌 🚊 to Porta Palazzo

Jana (4, J6)

This blindingly white space will at times seem more like a gallery for high-end fashion than a mere retailer. Find all the best and most innovative designs here, from those deconstructionist stalwart Martin Margiela to the wild-but-flawless technician Jean-Paul Gaultier, and let your credit card do the rest.

☎ 011 885 495
✉ Via Maria Vittoria 45a 🕓 3.30-7.30pm Mon, 9.30am-12.30pm & 3.30-7.30pm Tue-Sat
🚌 🚊 to Piazza Vittorio Veneto

Kristina Ti (4, G5)

This sublime exponent of women's fashion concentrates on imaginative styling, luxe fabrics and quirky details that allow the wearer to seem both à la mode *and* individual. There's a heavenly selection of lingerie and edible-looking shoes too, and the space itself is downright pretty. In case you're wondering, Kristina Ti is Turin born and bred.

☎ 011 837 170
✉ Via Maria Vittoria 18g
🕓 3.30-7.30pm Mon,

10am-2pm & 3.30-7.30pm Tue-Sat, 10am-7.30pm Thu 🚌 🚊 to Via Po

Massimo Rebecchi (4, E5)

Whoever Massimo is we love the velvety-soft knits, comfy pants, buttery leather jackets and smooth silk tops. Nothing here will jump out at you as 'right this second' in terms of fashion, but then again, you'll get to wear almost anything you buy here for a good five years without heading into outfit-update crisis mode.

☎ 011 517 82 55
✉ Via Gobetti 11
🕓 3.30-7.30pm Mon, 10am-1pm & 3.30-7.30pm Tue, Wed & Sat, 10am-7.30pm Thu & Fri
🚌 🚋 🚊 to Porta Nuova

Promosport (3, F7)

The best place to come for men's snowboarding gear and skatewear so that you can look as cool as possible on the slopes and streets. The idea of surfwear in Turin will generally make most non-Italians giggle, but there is a selection.

☎ 011 1950 22 49 ✉ Via Borromini 76 🕓 10am-12.30pm & 3.30-7.30pm Tue-Sat, 3.30-7.30pm Mon
🚊 3 🚌 30, 61

Rao (4, E5)

This stalwart of elegant dressing for men and women stocks luxurious cashmere sweaters, spiffy suits, hand-finished leather shoes and a dollop of pizzazz, so that you can be kitted out like a *La Dolce Vita* type in no time.

☎ 011 562 12 98
✉ cnr Via Lagrange & Via Camillo Cavour
🕓 3.30-7.30pm Mon, 10am-1pm & 3.30-7.30pm Tue, Wed, Fri & Sat, 10am-7.30pm Thu
🚌 🚊 to Via Lagrange

San Carlo dal 1913 (4, E3)

This modern emporium of all things labelled will have you afflicted with fashionitis in record time. Famous Italian names such as Gucci, Prada and the like compete for your attention and your wallet's commitment. Service is slick, and the gift-wrapping an art form. You can also find quirky little trinkets such as fragrant accessories for the home and children's books.

☎ 011 516 32 01 ✉ Via Roma 53 🕓 10am-7pm
🚌 🚊 to Piazza Castello

San Lorenzo (4, G5)

A large store that covers all the bases, from high-end fashion and accessories to surprisingly economical

CLOTHING & SHOE SIZES

Women's Clothing

Aust/UK	8	10	12	14	16	18
Europe	36	38	40	42	44	46
Japan	5	7	9	11	13	15
USA	6	8	10	12	14	16

Women's Shoes

Aust/USA	5	6	7	8	9	10
Europe	35	36	37	38	39	40
France only	35	36	38	39	40	42
Japan	22	23	24	25	26	27
UK	3½	4½	5½	6½	7½	8½

Men's Clothing

Aust	92	96	100	104	108	112
Europe	46	48	50	52	54	56

Japan	S	M	M		L	
UK/USA	35	36	37	38	39	40

Men's Shirts (Collar Sizes)

Aust/Japan	38	39	40	41	42	43
Europe	38	39	40	41	42	43
UK/USA	15	15½	16	16½	17	17½

Men's Shoes

Aust/UK	7	8	9	10	11	12
Europe	41	42	43	44½	46	47
Japan	26	27	27.5	28	29	30
USA	7½	8½	9½	10½	11½	12½

*Measurements approximate only;
try before you buy.*

gifts and homewares. It looks slick, but is actually an inviting, helpful and friendly shop, so don't feel scared, unless you're clumsy.

☎ 011 88 35 31
✉ Via des Ambrois 7
🕙 10am-1pm &
3.30-7.30pm Tue-Sat
🚌 🚋 to Piazza Castello

Seidiciluisaefranchino (4, E2)

Not only is this a hairdressing salon *(parrucchiere)*, it's also a neat place to find innovative, edgy fashion that breaks a few rules and has a bit of fun in the process. It's a hop, skip and jump from the markets at Porta Palazzo, but don't expect rock-bottom prices.

☎ 011 433 86 38
✉ Via IV Marzo 14a
🕙 10am-7pm Tue-Sat
🚌 🚋 to Porta Palazzo

Serienumerica (4, D1)

This spartan, modern space contains clothes reminiscent of 80s Commes des Garcons – ie lots of black and white interspersed with a burst of shocking colour and an almost origami-style approach to construction. Always interesting, and sure to make you stand out from the crowd.

☎ 011 436 96 44
✉ Via Sant' Agostino 23
🕙 3.30-8pm Tue-Thu, 3.30-8pm & 10.30-midnight Fri, 11am-1pm, & 3.30-8pm Sat
🚌 🚋 to Porta Palazzo

Shoeco (4, G4)

Shoeco, a bastion of style, showcases expensively subtle labels such as Dries Van Noten and Jil Sander, but also a pair of violet suede wedge-heeled shoes that we're *still* trying to convince ourselves we can wear as part of our workday. Service is helpful if you look like the sort of person whose bills are paid by someone else, or you don't look at price tags, period. Otherwise, you'll be pretty much invisible.

☎ 011 88 32 53
✉ Piazza Carlo Emanuele II 19 🕙 3.30-7.30pm Mon, 10am-1pm & 3.30-7.30pm Tue-Sat
🚌 🚋 to Piazza Castello

Get friendly with some shady Italians

ACCESSORIES

Bruschi (4, E4)

The brusque service at Bruschi brightens noticeably when it becomes obvious that you're as serious about the €250 Prada loafers as they are. Otherwise, expect to get short shrift if you're wearing less than your Sunday best or not carrying a lap dog, as you do.

☎ 011 562 55 46
✉ Piazza San Carlo 208
☼ 3.30-7.30pm Mon, 10am-7.30pm Tue-Fri, 9.30am-1pm & 3.30-7.30pm Sat 🚌 🚊 🚋 to Porta Nuova or Piazza Castello

Calzedonia (4,G4)

This cheap and cheerful chain store has all sorts of funky socks, stockings and pantyhose for legging it around town in style without breaking the bank. There are branches all over town, including on Piazza Statuto, Via Roma and Via Garibaldi.

☎ 011 817 49 39
✉ Via Po 10a
☼ 9.30am-12.30pm & 3-7pm 🚌 🚋 to Via Po

Creativity (4, G6)

Funky craft-style accessories can be found here, with a particularly good range of earrings, hats and scarves. Service is friendly, and more than willing to help the indecisive.

☎ 011 817 78 64 ✉ Via Mazzini 29e ☼ 10am-1pm & 3.30-7.30pm Tue-Sun 🚌 🚊 🚋 to Porta Nuova

Mandarina Duck (4, E5)

Mandarina Duck is an Italian firm with an international reputation for funky, modern bags and wallets in a range of interesting colours and shapes. Staff are extremely knowledgeable about all the bells and whistles on the various products, and will be glad to help you narrow down their selection until you're left with exactly the right bag or wallet.

☎ 011 54 73 66 ✉ Piazza CLN 259 ☼ 9am-12.30pm & 3.30-7.30pm Mon-Sat 🚌 🚊 🚋 to Porta Nuova

Leg it into Calzedonia

VINTAGE

Turin, unlike many Italian cities, has a fondness for old clothes and has a smattering of funky shops that cater to aficionados. You won't find thrift- or second-hand shops here, but you will find old duds with character.

J&S Vintage (4, J5)
This too-cool-for-school purveyor of vintage finds is the best place to come for pre-loved couture and designer frocks and party pieces. In fact, it's a bit of a party in itself, with *aperitivi* (aperitifs) served between 7pm and 9pm on Friday nights.
☎ 011 812 15 88
✉ Via Matteo Pescatore 11b ◷ 4-9pm Mon-Sat 🚌 🚊 to Piazza Vittorio Veneto

La Terra delle Donne (4, D1)
One of our faves – a dress-up box come to life, with wonderful pieces from the 18th century to the 1970s, and some very

decent prices. Find a perfect silk scarf to protect your hairdo or a stunning piece of antique lacework. Sweet service too.
☎ 347 418 13 08
✉ Via San Domenico 18 ◷ 9.30am-4pm Mon & Wed, 9.30am-12.30pm Tue, 9.30am-12.30pm & 3.30-7.30pm Thu & Fri, 10am-12.30pm Sat 🚌 🚊 to Piazza Castello or Porta Palazzo

Lo Zio d'America (4, E2)
'The American Uncle' is a retro clothes shop with what seems like a million velour tracksuit tops from the decade that taste forgot. A great place to rummage through the colour palette that starts at canary yellow

and ends at poo brown, and find out where many of the city's uni students are heading out to that night. Items from the 1950s and 60s can also be discovered if you look hard enough.
☎ 011 436 14 23
✉ Via Palazzo di Città 14 ◷ 3.30-7.30pm Mon, 11am-1pm & 3.30-7pm Tue-Sat 🚌 🚊 to Piazza Castello

Sticky Fingers (4, D1)
Any vintage clothing shop named after a classic Rolling Stones album gets a big (sticky) thumbs up from us. Carla, the owner, stocks three rooms' worth of pre-loved couture and flam-mable fabrics and is happy to let you play dress-ups

A milliner's masterpiece maybe?

Good Books

Local efforts that you may want to peruse include Natalia Ginzburg's *All Our Yesterdays*, Cesare Pavese's *Disaffections*, Primo Levi's *Other People's Trades* or any of the works of Alessandro Baricco published in English. Baricco has started a local 'writing school' of sorts, known as the Scuola Holden (after the protagonist from The *Catcher in the Rye*). If this sounds good, then *The Second Messiah: Templars*, *The Turin Shroud* and *The Great Secret of Freemasonry* by Christopher Knight and Robert Lomas will pique your interest.

while she and her pals gossip. Prices will seem quite high if you're used to vintage trawling in the UK, Australia, or US but you won't have to scour each garment for armpit stains and the shop is not at all claustrophobic or cramped.
☎ 011 521 73 20
✉ Via delle Orfane 24d
🕑 11am-2pm & 4-8pm
Tue-Sat 🚌 🚊 **to Porta Palazzo**

ART & ANTIQUES

Galleria Caretto (4, F4)

Do you have bare walls? Find the perfect 17th-century Flemish painting to adorn them here. Wonderful art and antiques abound – press the buzzer to enter a glorious time capsule of sorts. Not the sort of place for aimless browsing, but a good spot to pretend 'money is no object'.
☎ 011 53 72 74 🖥 www .galleriacaretto.com, **In Italian** ✉ **Via Maria Vittoria 10** 🕑 **9.45am-12.30pm & 4-7pm Tue-Sat** 🚌 🚊 **to Piazza Castello**

Galleria Gilibert

This gloriously beautiful bookshop is lined with rare books and prints in this prettiest of Turin's shopping arcades, the Galleria Subalpina (4, F3). Look for the window filled with cherubs and old books and press the doorbell to gain entry to this jewel of a shop.
☎ 011 561 92 25
✉ **Galleria Subalpina 17** 🕑 **9.30am-12.30pm & 5.30-7.30pm Tue-Sun** 🚌 🚊 **to Piazza Castello**

L'estampe (4, E2)

Lovely L'estampe specialises in loose illustrations, pages from illuminated manuscripts and old maps, making it an excellent place to find a unique souvenir. A few rare books are also available, but it's likely the interesting art prints will take your fancy. Service is extremely courteous and helpful and packing and shipping can be arranged.
☎ 011 561 28 01 ✉ **Via dei Mercanti 3g** 🕑 **3.30-7.30pm Mon, 10am-1pm & 3.30-7.30pm Tue-Sat** 🚌 🚊 **to Piazza Castello**

Marco Polo Antichitá (4, H5)

If the early 19th century was your era, then this is the antique store you should frequent – although you can also find some excellent pieces from the 18th century too. Owners Oreste and Angelo are happy to explain the provenance of each item of furniture.
☎ 011 817 77 82 ✉ **Via Principe Amedeo 52** 🕑 **9.30am-12.30pm &**

3.30-7.30pm Tue-Sat, 3.30-7.30pm Mon 🚌 🚊 **to Piazza Vittorio Veneto**

Memorie del Passato

Dealer Alessandro Macri's delightful store in Galleria Subalpina (4, F3) is full of Art Nouveau, Liberty and Jugendstil pieces and antique fabrics. Everything sold here comes with a certificate of authenticity, and Alessandro is friendly and fluent in English, so don't be shy!
☎ 011 562 26 45
✉ **Galleria Subalpina 18** 🕑 **10.15am-12.45pm & 3.30-7.45pm Tue-Sat** 🚌 🚊 **to Piazza Castello**

Stile Floreale (4, F4)

This delightful antique store is very certain of where its talents lie – in the early 20th century. Expect to find furniture and beautiful jewellery that exemplifies the best in Art Nouveau, Art Deco and, of course, Liberty.
☎ 011 817 04 21
✉ **Via Maria Vittoria 19** 🕑 **9.30am-12.30pm & 3.30-7.30pm Tue-Sat** 🚌 🚊 **to Piazza Castello**

RETRO & HOMEWARES

There are plenty of fabulous stores specialising in funky post-war furnishings in Turin.

Arredo 7 (4, D2)
Arredo 7 stocks funky little knick-knacks and objets from another era – and will have you nostalgic for the days of orange-hued everything and innovative plastic shapes. Stock up on swingin' artefacts for your bachelor pad with plenty of friendly advice and reasonable price tags.
☎ 011 53 97 42 ✉ Via Barbaroux 20d ✆ 3.30-7.30pm Mon, 10.30am-1pm & 3.30-7.30pm Tue-Sat 🚌 🚈 to Piazza Castello

Galleria Giancarlo Cristiani (4, J5)
A wonderful spot to find homewares and furnishings from the 20th century that are in uniformly excellent condition. Items are sourced from both Italy and overseas, and range in size from things you can fit in your suitcase to the headache-inducingly large.
☎ 011 817 83 91 🖥 www.cristiani.net ✉ Via Maria Vittoria 41g ✆ 10am-12.30pm & 3.30-7.30pm Tue-Sat, 3.30-7.30pm Mon 🚌 🚈 to Piazza Castello or Piazza Vittorio Veneto

Marco Cappello Arte e Design (4, E2)
Marco's moody-looking space has some fabulous finds from the best of the late 20th century, including a large Campbell's soup-can stool. Opening hours are limited, but you can call to

---

Choc-full of Happiness

Turin's best-known confectioner, **Leone**, has been making sweets since 1857. Favourites include fruity bonbons inscribed with the word *allegria* (meaning 'happiness') on the outer wrapper; old-fashioned 'matchboxes' filled with tiny *pastiglie* (lozenges) in mint, mandarin and myriad other flavours; and its gold-wrapped *gianduja* (delicious smooth hazelnut chocolate). Historic shops selling Leone bonbons, chocolates and jellied fruits include **Pasticceria Fratelli Stratta** (4, E4; Piazza San Carlo 191), founded in 1836; **Abrate** (4, G4; Via Po 12a), with its lovely 1920s shop; and **Avvignano** (4, D6; Piazza Carlo Felice 50), founded in 1883 and known for its *sorrisi di Torino* (literally, 'smiles from Turin').

---

arrange an appointment if your time is tight.
☎ 011 436 12 45 ✉ Via Palazzo di Città 21b ✆ 4-7pm Tue-Sat 🚌 🚈 to Piazza Castello or Porta Palazzo

Marco Modernariato (4, J5)
Bright furniture and furnishing objects leap out at you in this funky store devoted to post-war decorating. Expect rarities and various gems that bring on nostalgia as you stumble upon something from your past.
☎ 011 812 97 42 🖥 www.marcomodern ariato.com ✉ Via della Rocca 2m ✆ 9.30am-7.30pm Tue-Sat, 3.30-7.30pm Mon 🚌 🚈 to Via Po

Marco Polo (4, D1)
Hard-to-define Marco Polo is one of the city's trendy

new spots, where every customer seems to be in the throes of making sure their lifestyle is, well, stylish. You can drink here, dine here, have brunch here (€14) and pick up another scented candle, another generously proportioned sofa, another knick-knack.
☎ 011 436 00 37 ✉ Via Sant'Agostino 28 ✆ 10am-8.30pm Tue & Wed, 10am-midnight Thu-Sat, 3.30-7.30pm Mon, café 8am-11pm Tue-Thu, 8am-2am Sat, noon-4pm Sun 🚌 🚈 to Porta Palazzo

Miscellanea (4, D1)
At times, Miscellanea feels more like a friend's bedroom on a Saturday night. You're trying on outfits, classic rock (Stooges, Stones etc) is blaring from the record player, you're joking about what you're going

to get up to later. A great, relaxed shop crammed with clothes, homewares and stuff that can't really be categorised, except to say that the name of the shop is spot-on.
☎ 339 797 40 16
✉ Via San Domenico 6d
🕓 11am-10pm Tue-Sat
🚌 🚃 to Porta Palazzo or Piazza Castello

Turin Gallery (4, F4)
Worth a visit even if you're not intending to buy, this veritable Aladdin's cave of 20th-century design classics is filled to bursting point with wacky furniture, col-ourful glassware and *objets d'art*. Styles range from the sublime to the avant-garde, from the elegant to the somewhat barmy.

A highlight piece is a pouf shaped like an upturned bowler hat filled with an apple entitled *Homage to Magritte* designed by Dino Gavina.
☎ 011 812 30 83
✉ Via Maria Vittoria 19 🕓 9.30am-1pm & 3-7pm Mon-Sat
🚌 🚃 to Piazza Castello

MUSIC & BOOKS

Feltrinelli (4, E4)
This branch of the well-regarded Italian bookshop chain stocks a decent range of Lonely Planet guides (in English and Italian) and plenty of coffee table books that will have you cursing airline baggage restrictions.
☎ 011 534 914
✉ Via Roma 80
🕓 8am-7.30pm Mon-Thu, 8am-11pm Fri & Sat, 8.30am-1pm & 4-7pm Sun
🚌 🚃 to Piazza Castello

FNAC (4, E3)
Big branch of the French chain, with books, CDs, DVDs and lots of electronic equipment, plus ticketing and Internet access, and a handy café.
☎ 011 551 67 11
✉ Via Roma 56
🕓 9.30am-8pm Mon-Sat, 10am-8pm Sun
🚌 🚃 to Piazza Castello

Libreria Dante Alighieri (4, D6)
This delightful bookshop

has enough seating for you to settle in with one of their art books and forget about a rainy day outside. It's a charming space, crammed with titles in an old-fashioned building and is blessed with tons of character.
☎ 011 53 58 97
✉ Piazza Carlo Felice 15 🕓 3-7.30pm Mon, 9.30am-7.30pm Tue-Sat, 10.30am-1.30pm Sun
🚌 🚃 🚃 to Porta Nuova

No need for shushing here

A fair indication of what you'll find at Via Bogino 4

Ricordi Media Store (4, E5)

A good solid mainstream choice for CDs of all genres: rock, pop, classical, Italian, international and more. It also sells tickets for concerts.
☎ 011 562 11 56
✉ Piazza CLN 251
🕓 9am-7.30pm Mon-Sat, 10am-1pm & 3.30-7.30pm Sun 🚌 🚊 🚋 to Porta Nuova

Libreria Luxemburg (4, F3)

This friendly, helpful bookshop stocks a choice range of Italian and foreign books plus glossy international magazines in case you're feeling like something a little less ponderous.
☎ 011 561 38 96
✉ Via Battisti 7
🕓 8am-7.30pm
🚌 🚋 to Piazza Castello

Mood (4, F3)

A slick range of arty tomes, glorious cookbooks and glossy coffee table books begs to be perused at this modern bookshop, which has a good café attached to it (see p69).
☎ 011 566 08 09
✉ Via Battisti 3e
🕓 10am-9pm Mon-Sat
🚌 🚋 to Piazza Castello

Rock & Folk (4, F4)

A good spot to source indie and alternative music releases and find out who's playing where, as the staff are young and clued-up.
☎ 011 839 45 42 ✉ Via Bogino 4 🕓 9.30am-2pm & 3.30-7.30pm Tue-Sat, 3.30-7.30pm Mon 🚌 🚋 to Piazza Castello

SPECIALIST & QUIRKY STORES

Aromaticobar (4, E3)

We can't resists a store that smells this good! Hard-to-find perfume brands from around the world and interesting grooming supplies, especially for men with tough beards.
☎ 011 54 01 41
✉ Via San Tommaso 7
🕓 10am-7.30pm Tue-Fri, 3.30-7.30pm Mon & Sat
🚌 🚋 to Piazza Castello

Juventus Store (4, E2)

Turin's most famous football team has a store dedicated to letting its many fans score a little piece of the action – a strip will set you back about €70 and give you something to wear to Sunday's game at the Stadio delle Alpi. You can also get balls here.

☎ 011 433 87 09 ✉ Via Giuseppe Garibaldi 4 🕓 3-7.30pm Mon, 10am-7.30pm Tue-Sat 🚌 🚋 to Piazza Castello

Legolibri (4, H5)

Devotees of the social sciences, psychology and psychoanalysis will want to hightail it down to this

This store always runs in the black (and white)

The traditional Juventus top (right), and the mysteriously fewer-selling pink version

bookshop, where too much theory is barely enough, and the rapid-fire debates flow thick and fast. Don't forget to pack your Freudian slip.

☎ 011 88 89 75
✉ Via Maria Vittoria 31
🕐 9.30am-1pm & 3.30-7.30pm Tue, Wed, Fri & Sat, 9.30am-7.30pm Thu, 3.30-7.30pm Mon
🚍 🚊 to Via Po

Olympic Store (4, E2)
Crammed with all sorts of official Olympic souvenirs stamped with various logos and brands, from the cute mascots Gliz and Neve to some cringe-worthy winter knits. Other branches can be found at Atrium in Piazza Solferino and at the airport.

🖥 www.olympicstore
.it ✉ Via Giuseppe Garibaldi 6 🕐 9am-7pm
Tue-Sat 🚍 🚊 to Piazza Castello

Pellerino (4, E3)
So what if email has commandeered the written word! This lovely store stocks a lifetime's worth of paper cuts, and has been going strong for over 100 years.

☎ 011 53 53 96
✉ Via Mercanti 11
🕐 9.30am-12.30pm & 3.30-7pm Tue-Sat, 3.30-7pm Mon 🚍 🚊 to Piazza Castello

Profumeria Borgonuovo (4, H6)
This enchanting shop stocks wonderful boutique scents and brands such as Etro, Penhaligon and that old Italian staple, fabulous Acqua di Parma. You can also find cosmetics and that near-ubiquitous symbol of the times, the scented candle.

☎ 011 812 43 81 ✉ Via della Rocca 10c 🕐 10am-1pm & 3.30-7.30pm Tue-Sat 🚍 🚊 to Piazza Vittorio Veneto

Christmas Spirit

If the festive season is a year-round pleasure for you then a visit to **La Bottega di Natale** (4, D3; ☎ 011 53 17 64; Via Mercanti 8e; 🕐 10am-1pm & 3-7pm Tue-Sat, 3-7pm Mon, extra from mid-Nov to 24 Dec) is a must. All sorts of Christmas decorations, *presepe* (nativity scenes) and festive objects are crammed into this extraordinary shop. Atheists and cynics should steer well clear.

FOOD & DRINK

Borgiattino Formaggi (3, B6)

One thousand and one nights' worth of cheese dreams from the store (going since 1927) with what seems like one thousand and one different types of cheese. Unmissable – we'd put this in the Highlights chapter if we were sure everyone would fit.

☎ 011 55 38 37
✉ Corso Vinzaglio 29
🕑 8.30am-1pm & 4-7.30pm Mon, Tue & Thu-Sat 🚌 29, 55, 72 🚋 13

Gertosio (4, E6)

Pop in here to stock up on bread (savoury, fruit or sugar-topped) and other lip-smacking baked goods. If you're interested and have a devil-may-care attitude to dental cavities, you can also get 50 different types of praline here.

☎ 011 562 19 42 ✉ Via Lagrange 34 🕑 8am-7.30pm Tue-Sat, 8am-1pm Sun 🚌 🚋 🚋 to Porta Nuova

Pastificio de Filippis (4, E6)

A gastronomic delight, De Filippis sells every type of pasta under the Italian sun. Specialities include tortellini stuffed with fillings such as spinach, salmon and *fonduta* (a type of melted cheese from Valle d'Aosta); artichokes, asparagus, eggplant and mushrooms; or ham, walnuts and gorgonzola.

☎ 011 542 21 37 ✉ Via Lagrange 39 🕑 9am-12.30pm & 3-7.30pm

Start Wining

For details on Piedmont's prodigious wine industry, contact the **Enoteca del Piemonte** (6, A5; ☎ 011 667 76 67; www.enotecadelpiemonte.com; Via Nizza 294), the central office representing the region's 10 wine cellars.

Tue-Sat, 3-7.30pm Mon 🚌 🚋 🚋 to Porta Nuova

Peyrano (4, B5)

Peyrano, the creator of *dolci momenti a Torino* (sweet moments in Turin) and *grappini* (chocolates filled with grappa), is Turin's most-famous chocolate house. And rightly so. Buy one of everything – you know you want to – or drop by here first for a gift if you've been invited to Sunday lunch at someone's house.

☎ 011 53 87 65
✉ Corso Vittorio Emanuele II 76

🕑 9.30am-8pm Tue-Sat, 9.30am-1pm Sun 🚌 🚋 🚋 to Porta Nuova

Rossorubino (5, B2)

This is an excellent new *enoteca* (wine bar) where you can sample wines but also socialise or dine in attractive surrounds. It's located in the rejuvenated area known as Sal Salvario, and has a large selection (well over 500) of local wines to choose from.

☎ 011 650 21 83
✉ Via Madama Cristina 21a 🕑 10.30am-9pm Tue-Sat 🚋 18 🚌 67

Choc til you drop at Peyrano

Eating

Turin is the sort of city that leaves her visitors with the impression that locals think about little else other than their next meal. Perhaps it's the tendency towards hard work that has led to such an appetite, but one thing's for sure – you won't be going hungry in this town. With a gourmet culture as well defined as Piedmont's, eating in the region's capital is taken *very* seriously. Michelin-starred chefs compete with family-run trattorias, and pizzerias vie with ethnic eateries to satisfy the demands of a highly discerning public – who all have an opinion on where to eat, what to eat and what to drink with it and when. There are some 800-odd places to eat in Turin – following are some of our favourites.

You can find route numbers for transport on p114.

Meal Costs

These prices are for two courses and a drink, but bear in mind that up to €10 refers to eating a quick snack or a pizza with a drink, rather than a sit-down meal in a restaurant proper.

$	up to €10
$$	€11-25
$$$	€26-40
$$$$	over €41

Turin's Cuisine

Delicate and flavoursome, Piedmont cuisine fuses the very best of French and Italian gastronomy. Restaurant menus are often determined by produce availability at the local market, and relationships with various suppliers of meat, fish and poultry are assiduously cultivated to ensure that only the best reaches your table. Meaty local specialities include *bollito misto* (seven types of sauce-topped, broth-boiled meat), *finanziera* (sweetbreads, mushrooms and chicken livers in a creamy sauce), *brasato al Barolo* (braised beef, marinated in aged Barolo wine) and, in a gesture of good will to vegetarians who eat fish, *bagna cauda* (raw vegetables dipped fondue-style in a sauce of garlic, red wine and melted anchovies)

While Turin is quite a multicultural city, the eating scene only partially reflects this, with some good Indian, Japanese and Middle-Eastern restaurants and the usual roster of rather indifferent Chinese joints.

Opening Hours

Restaurants generally open from 12.30pm to 2.30pm and then again from 7.30pm to 11pm and close for one day each week (often Monday or Tuesday).

Turin's speciality, classy cafés

IL CENTRO

The city centre offers plenty of choice, from some of the city's swishest gastrodomes that encourage lingering over just one more dish or drink, to convenient pit-stops catering to office workers wanting sustenance on a budget and in a tight timeframe.

Al Garamond (4, F5) $$$$
Piedmontese
One of the city's best restaurants, Al Garamond is an elegant example of how tradition and creativity can combine to form something truly special. The fish dishes are highly recommended, and the wine list is excellent. A wonderful choice for an important business lunch, where you want to make sure that everything is 'just so'.
☎ 011 812 27 81 ✉ Via Pomba 14 🕑 12.30-2.30pm & 8-10.30pm Mon-Fri, 8-10.30pm Sat 🚌 🚋 🚎 to Porta Nuova

Arcadia $$$
Piedmontese & Japanese
When you feel like local food and your travelling companion is craving sushi you can reach a compromise at Arcadia, located in the beautiful Galleria Subalpina (4, F3). It's a large, rather formal restaurant that proves popular at lunch with smart-looking types and the sushi is very good indeed, thanks to the Japanese chef who helped

establish this – the first sushi bar in the city.
☎ 011 561 38 98 ✉ Galleria Subalpina 16 🕑 noon-2pm & 7.30-10.30pm Mon-Sat 🚌 🚎 to Piazza Castello

Brek (4, D5) $
Fast Food
Italy's very luxurious version of fast food is a quick stumble from the train station and heaves at lunchtime. Its interior courtyard beats many of Turin's restaurants' outside dining areas in the charm stakes.
☎ 011 53 45 56 ✉ Piazza Carlo Felice 10 🕑 11.30am-3pm & 6.30-10.30pm 🚌 🚋 🚎 to Porta Nuova

El Centenario (4, C5) $$
Tex-Mex
This is a good place to frequent if you simply can't face another *bollito misto*, with all the usual Tex-Mex staples and even a children's menu (not a common thing in Turin). The décor is cheery and suitably Latino in tone, with late opening hours appropriate for a

sometimes *mañana* style of service.
☎ 011 54 15 59 ✉ Via Biancamano 3 🕑 7.30pm-2am 🚌 to Piazza Solferino or 🚌 🚋 🚎 to Porta Nuova

Ekky (4, D5) $
Fast Food
Ekky is an excellent spot for a healthy meal on the run at very reasonable prices. You'll find plenty of freshly prepared salads (named after capital cities), baguettes (named after writers) and *ciabatte* (named after actresses) and lots of local and international newspapers to read. It's spotlessly clean too.
☎ 011 560 41 08 ✉ cnr Via XX Settembre & Via Gramsci 🕑 8am-2am Mon-Thu, 8am-9pm Fri & Sat 🚌 🚋 🚎 to Porta Nuova

Il Punto Verde (4, G5) $$
Vegetarian
Turin is a carnivorous city, so vegetarians will be grateful for this, one of the few exclusively animal-friendly eateries in town. There are various menu options to choose from, as well as a selection of *monopiatti* (single dishes) for less than €10. A decent lunchtime option.
☎ 011 88 55 43 ✉ Via San Massimo 17 🕑 12.30-2.30pm Mon-Sat 🚌 🚎 to Via Po

---

Lights Out
In January 2005 Italy introduced a ban on smoking in public places. You can no longer light up in bars or restaurants unless there is a separate, closed-off smoking area.

Kiki (5, D1) $$$
Japanese
Hip and modern, this beautiful Japanese restaurant gets packed with Turin's trendy set who flirt madly at the communal table while doing their level best to master the art of eating with chopsticks. A damn fine list of sake and Japanese beers lubricates both efforts.
☎ 011 83 50 84 ✉ Via della Rocca 39g ☽ noon-2.30pm & 7.30-10pm Tue-Sun 🚋 🚇 to Piazza Vittorio Veneto

Kirkuk Kafé (4, F4) $$
Middle Eastern
Sit cross-legged on the silk cushions and tuck into the Kurdish, Turkish, Iraqi and Iranian fare served up at this perennially popular eatery. The food is pretty good, the service informal, and for the stiffer-limbed there are traditional tables and chairs. You'll need to book for dinner, and arrive relatively early at lunch.
☎ 011 53 06 57 ✉ Via Carlo Alberto 16bis ☽ 6.30pm-midnight Mon, Tue & Sat, noon-3pm & 6.30pm-midnight Wed-Fri 🚋 🚇 to Piazza Castello

L'Agrifoglio (5, C1) $$$
Piedmontese
Small but perfectly formed, L'Agrifoglio is the sort of much-loved restaurant that encourages you to make a reservation, as it's extremely popular for its modern twists on stalwart regional dishes. The wine list is as robust as the flavours emanating from the kitchen,

and features around 250 choices. For an antipasto, try the splendid *capunet*.
☎ 011 83 70 64 ✉ Via Academia Albertina 38d ☽ 8pm-midnight Tue-Sat 🚋 🚇 🚇 to Porta Nuova

La Badessa (4, G5) $$$
Monastic
La Badessa means Mother Superior in Italian, and the quasi-religious overtones of this charming restaurant (they describe the cooking as 'monastic') will have you giving thanks to the higher power at the stove. In summer, tables spill out onto the delightful piazza, but even if you're seated indoors you'll appreciate the charming interior, decorated with portraits of religious types. A restaurant so good we'll even forgive the mortal sin of making the waiter wear a priest's collar.
☎ 011 83 59 40 ✉ Piazza Carlo Emanuele II 17h ☽ 12.30-2.30pm & 8-11pm Tue-Sat, 8-11pm Mon 🚋 🚇 to Piazza Castello

La Vitel Etonné (4, G4) $$
Piedmontese
This small, welcoming spot boasts an excellent

wine cellar and local favourite *vitello tonnato* (cold roast veal with tuna, mayonnaise and capers). Portions are excellent for lunching – just enough to leave you satisfied, not so much that you'll need your waistband altered. After your meal, cleanse your palate (and your sinuses) with a *sorbetto* made from rockmelon and *pepperoncino* (chilli).
☎ 011 812 46 21 ✉ Via San Francesco da Paola 4 ☽ 12.30-3pm & 8.30-10.30pm Mon, Tue & Thu-Sat, 12.30-3pm Wed & Sun 🚋 🚇 to Piazza Castello

Mood (4, F3) $
Bookshop Café
This slickly modern bookshop sports a cool café that makes for the perfect spot to browse through glossy coffee-table tomes while grazing on such fare as *fagottini ripieni di formaggio con speck e zucchine* (fagottini stuffed with cheese, speck and zucchini) or the *insalata mood* (home salad).
☎ 011 566 08 09 ✉ Via Battisti 3e ☽ café 8am-9pm Mon-Sat, shop 10am-9pm Mon-Sat 🚋 🚇 to Piazza Castello

---

Tic Tac Toe

You may well associate Turin with fine dining titbits such as *bagna cauda, fonduta* and *bollito misto*, all washed down with fabulous velvety-soft reds, but did you also know that you can well and truly finish off your meal with another Turin speciality? The Tic Tac is the city's gift to fresh, post-prandial breath, and probably the lowest-joule thing you'll get close to in this slow-food lovin' town.

Days of Wine
Keep your eyes peeled for restaurants advertising the fact that they are *'butastupa'* establishments. This means that they will gladly let you take any unfinished wine from your bottle home with you. Apparently some people don't get through the whole thing in one sitting…

Posto (4, E6) $$$
Italian
Sleek, modern and possessed of a communal table (unusual for Italian joints), this is a fashionable, popular spot with a busy bar attached (it opens from 8am to midnight), which often features DJ sounds. The enormous feature wall that sports a picture of a glacier need not inspire a sense of foreboding – this place is cool, but not frosty. Try the *piatto etnico del giorno* (ethnic plate of the day – €15).
☎ 011 566 07 09
✉ Via Lagrange 34
🕐 12.30-2.30pm & 7.30-10.30pm Mon-Sat 🚌 to Via Lagrange

Ristorante Carignano $$$$
Piedmontese
This beautifully old-fashioned restaurant, located in the Grand Hotel Sitea (4, E5), specialises in Piedmontese classics, but also turns an expert hand to more international cuisine, all accompanied by a very good wine list. Dress the part – lest you look less impressive than the sometimes elaborate desserts that resemble works of art.
☎ 011 517 01 71
✉ Via Carlo Alberto 35 🕐 12.30-2.30pm & 7.30-10.30pm Mon-Fri & Sun, 7.30-10.30pm Sat 🚌 🚋 to Piazza Castello

Ristorante del Cambio (4, F3) $$$$
Italian
Dripping in history (founded in 1753), the stylish lunchtime bolt-hole of no less than Cavour (whose regular *posto* – seat – is marked by a plaque) is a famous and popular place for Turin's well-heeled and well-connected politicians and business types to conduct business. Anything on the menu is worth trying, although we were particularly impressed by the *sogliola grigliata alle erbe aromatiche* (grilled sole with aromatic herbs – €21) and the €6.40 per gram truffle shavings that can accompany most dishes. We were less impressed, however, with the 15% service charge – although the service *is* politically correct.
☎ 011 54 37 60
✉ Piazza Carignano 2 🕐 12.30-2.30pm & 8-10.30pm Mon-Sat 🚌 🚋 to Piazza Castello

You're unlikely to be scowling when you leave Ristorante del Cambio

Ristorante Vintage 1997 (4, C4) $$$$

Mediterranean

The gold-and-gilt laden Michelin-starred extravaganza that is Vintage 1997 continues to win rave reviews from the lucky gourmands who frequent it. Still so hot it scorches, the rapturous reception that greeted it upon its opening a few years ago shows no sign of abating. Expect inventive Italian and Mediterranean cuisine (the seafood main courses are from heaven) and a fabulous wine list. Two degustation menus are available – one with eight small courses (€45), one with 13 (€65). Reservations essential.

☎ 011 53 59 48
✉ Piazza Solferino 16h
🕑 noon-3pm & 8-11pm Mon-Fri, 8-11pm Sat
🚌 to Piazza Solferino

Take a delivery of some Michelin-starred food

Sileno (4, D3) $$

Italian

The starkly minimalist décor of Sileno belies the fact that you'll find traditional comfort food (minestrone, roast meat etc) at incredibly reasonable prices at this newish eatery. At lunch, you can choose from simple menus that cost between €6.50 and €13 (the latter includes first and second courses, plus a side dish, dessert and some water). It's a little noisy (the floor, covered in white stones, seems to allow every word to ricochet a few times), but it's also welcoming and informal.

☎ 011 53 58 80
✉ Via Monte di Pietà 23 🕑 12.30-3pm &

7.30-11pm Tue-Sun
🚌 to Piazza Solferino or
🚌 🚋 to Piazza Castello

Societé Lutéce (4, G4) $$

Brunch

On sunny days, the terrace here (overlooking delightful Piazza Carlo Emanuele II) is one of the places to be seen. Inside is suitably retro and attractive, and the weekend brunches are wonderful.

☎ 011 88 76 44 ✉ Piazza Carlo Emanuele II 21
🕑 12.30-4pm Tue-Sun
🚌 🚋 to Piazza Castello

Stars & Roses (4, D6) $$

Pizzeria

Relative newcomer Stars & Roses goes all out in trying to make an impression via celebrity pictures and a bold use of colour. Downstairs pizzas are served in the sunny orange room, while upstairs stylish greys and blacks predominate. The menu

ranges from the classic to the boldly outrageous – think Margherita, then think a topping with caviar and vodka.

☎ 011 516 20 52
✉ Piazza Paleocapa 2d 🕑 noon-3pm & 7pm-1am Tue-Sat
🚌 🚋 🚋 to Porta Nuova

Tobiko (4, D4) $$

Japanese

Stripped right back to its barest Japanese essentials, this tranquil eating space serves good-value *bento* boxes and has a nifty little sushi bar. No-one will look askance if you ask for a knife and fork either, or if you ask for something to take away.

☎ 011 53 79 23 ✉ Via Alfieri 20 🕑 noon-3pm & 8-11pm Tue-Sun
🚌 to Piazza Solferino or
🚌 🚋 to Piazza Castello

QUADRILATERO ROMANO

The city's coolest and most historic quarter is crammed with interesting places to eat and imbibe – often at the same time. Our listings here also include restaurants in the Borgo Dora, across Corso Regina Margherita.

AB+ (4, E1) $$$
Creative Mediterranean
Chef Alessandro Boglione's magnificent culinary creations warrant being listed as a highlight of a visit to Turin. In a modern, beautiful space filled with modern, beautiful people it's impossible not to be captivated by dishes such as *costolette di agnello con croccante kataifi con salsa di lardo e menta e carciofi stufati* (essentially lamb cutlet with artichoke). Book a table, and don't leave it until you've had three courses (make one a *fassone* – beef – dish if you're a carnivore) and something from the great wine list. The restaurant is attached to a hotel; for information on the hotel, see p97.
☎ 011 439 06 18
✉ Via della Basilica 13
🕑 6pm-1am Mon-Sat
🚌 🚃 to Porta Palazzo

Al Andalus (3, D5) $$
Middle Eastern
Turin's *hammam* (Turkish bathhouse) also possesses a fine restaurant, with a range of dishes from places such as Syria and Morocco, including *tabouleh*, *felafel* and the like. The experience is best shared with a group and washed down with lots of mint tea.
☎ 011 521 64 96 ✉ Via Fiochetto 15 🕑 noon-2pm & 8-11pm Mon-Sat
🚌 🚃 to Porta Palazzo

Worth the Trip

Combal.Zero (2, B2) $$$$
Modern Italian
Setting, style and substance form a Davide Scabin–created *ménage à trois* to remember at this wonderful Michelin-starred restaurant that runs the length of the *manica lunga* (long sleeve) of the Castello di Rivoli. Everything, from the stemware to the T-shirt-clad staff, is perfect, and the excitement of cracking open the famous 'cyberegg' (€35; a cellophane-enclosed folly of caviar, vodka, egg yolk, shallots and pepper that you puncture with your own scalpel) is hard to beat, although the no-fuss pleasure of a risotto tinted with saffron and topped with black truffles is timeless too. The degustation menus cost €70, €80 or €140. Reservations essential.
☎ 011 956 52 25 ✉ Piazza Mafalda di Savoia, Rivoli 🕑 noon-2pm & 8-10pm Wed-Sun 🚌 36, then 36/ 🚕 taxi about €25 each way

Interior of Combal.Zero restaurant at Rivoli

Cantine Barbaroux (4, D2) $$

Italian

Possessed of one of the city's oldest wine cellars, this lovely *cantina con cucina* (wine cellar with kitchen) is not only an excellent spot to grab a hearty bowl of pasta or Tuscan bean soup, it's also a delightful spot to meet friends for a glass of wine or an *aperitivo* when the socialising starts in earnest. Note its red-brick, chequered tile cellar (original) and then get down to chatting with the friendly fellow customers that surround you.

☎ 011 53 54 12 ✉ Via Barbaroux 13f 🕑 noon-3pm & 6pm-2am Mon-Sat 🚌 🚊 to Piazza Castello

Casa Martin (4, D1) $$

Piedmontese

The city's coolest street boasts a number of fine eateries, including the romantic candlelit Casa Martin, which also has a delightful internal courtyard. Service is friendly and helpful, and you can have any of the dishes explained to you in English. Like many eateries in this neck of the woods, it's a popular drinking spot too, hence the long opening hours.

☎ 011 436 22 09 ✉ Via Sant'Agostino 23m 🕑 7pm-3am Tue-Sun 🚌 🚊 to Via XX Settembre or Via Milano

Diciottobi (4,E2) $$

Italian

The relaxed atmosphere at Diciottobi extends to its décor, which features

mismatched tables and chairs and a slightly scuffed ambience, despite the presence of a bold red feature wall. On Sundays between noon and 3pm a help-yourself brunch attracts a crowd, but at other times it's a straightforward Italian menu that keeps groups and arty types coming back. A very decent salad selection will tempt vegetarians.

☎ 011 436 25 83 ✉ Piazza Corpus Domini 18b 🕑 noon-3pm & 8-11pm Tue-Sun 🚌 🚊 to Piazza Castello

Fratelli La Cozza (3, E5) $$

Pizzeria

The last word in wacky, this incredibly popular place does Neapolitan-style pizza (and pasta dishes) and resembles a rather bizarre Tarantino-esque film set (giant plastic peppers, glass chandeliers etc). If you can't be bothered crossing the Dora to eat here, try the new branch at **Via Cesare Battisti 13** (4, F3; just near Piazza Carlo Alberto).

☎ 011 85 99 00 ✉ Corso Regio Parco 39 🕑 12.30-2.30pm & 7.30-midnight 🚌 19, 68

Gennaro Esposito (4, A1) $

Pizzeria

Even St Gennaro, the patron saint of Naples, would approve of the authentic pizzas here, which attract legions of fans – making reservations essential. There are just over 25 types of pizza to choose from but,

as is often the case, it's generally the simplest and most traditional that are the best.

☎ 011 53 59 05 ✉ Via Passalacqua 1g 🕑 12.15-2.30pm & 7.15pm-midnight Mon-Sat 🚌 🚊 to Piazza Statuto or 🚌 🚊 🚊 to Porta Susa

Il Bacaro (4, D1) $$$

Venetian

Featuring a warren-like and inviting interior, this is a charming spot to enjoy Venetian-influenced cuisine or a low-key drink before dinner. Indoor chairs can take the form of old train seats (and serve as loveseats to young couples) while the outdoor seats invite you to take full advantage of a sunny day (blankets are provided should the sun fail to appear). A terrific little hidey-hole on one of the city's best *piazze*.

☎ 011 436 90 64 ✉ Piazza della Consolata 1 🕑 noon-2am Tue-Sun 🚌 52, 60

Il Bagatto (4, D1) $$

Italian

This popular late opener fronts up against famous Tre Galli and offers a range of Italian staples and a groaning table of snacks and nibbles for the *aperitivo* hour. Its wine list is long and its degustation menu (€14) a bargain. Ochre-coloured walls add a warm touch.

☎ 011 436 88 87 ✉ Via Sant'Agostino 30a 🕑 5pm-2am Tue-Sun 🚌 🚊 to Via XX Settembre or Via Milano

I Scream, You Scream, We all Scream for Ice Cream…

The Torinese have bestowed legend status on a handful of its many *gelaterie* (ice-cream parlours).

- **Caffe Florio & Gelateria Florio** (4, G3; ☎ 011 817 32 25; Via Po 8) Nationalist haunt of Count Cavour, this place opened for business in 1780 and has been doling out stunning scoops ever since.
- **Pepino** (4, F4; ☎ 011 54 20 09; Piazza Carignano 8) Since 1884, people have been parading around this historic *gelateria* clutching *pinguini* (penguins) – ice cream on a stick covered with chocolate.
- **Caffé Miretti** (4, C5; ☎ 011 53 36 87; Corso Giacomo Matteoti 5) A wonderful range of flavours will have the indecisive in knots. If our opinion counts, we can't fault the orange cream flavour. In summer, the sunny pavement terrace is *de rigueur*.
- **Gatsby's** (4, E5; ☎ 011 562 25 45; Via Soleri 2) Swish, stylish and a fabulous spot to feast on vanilla and strawberry ice cream doused in champagne.
- **GROM** (4, D6; ☎ 011 511 90 67; Piazza Paleocapa 1d) A relatively new kid on the ice-cream block and winning rave reviews for its ice creams made with fab ingredients such as Sicilian pistachios and Guatemalan cocoa.

Get the scoop on Turin's coolest desserts at Caffe Florio & Gelateria Florio

La Focacceria Tipica Ligure (4, D2) $

Fast Food

There are a number of branches located around town of this convenient purveyor of *farinata* (a traditional Ligurian focaccia), for which you can choose from over a dozen different toppings. You can also buy pizza by the slice, making this a handy spot for munch-on-the-move options that won't hurt the hip pocket.

☎ 011 53 01 85

✉ Via Sant'Agostino 6

☽ 11am-8pm 🚌 🚇 to Piazza Castello

Marhaba (4, D1) $$

Middle Eastern

This attractive eating space specialises in Egyptian and other Middle Eastern cuisines and is extremely popular thanks to a combination of quality and centrality. It's probably the best option of its kind in this part of the world, and reservations are a good idea, especially if you fancy eating in the room with low tables, cushions and the *narghila* (water pipe).

☎ 011 521 44 52

✉ Via San Domenico 12 ☽ noon-3pm & 6pm-midnight Mon-Thu, 6pm-midnight Fri, noon-midnight Sat & Sun 🚌 🚃 to Piazza Castello

Montagne Viva (3, D5) $$$
Piedmontese
Traditionalists will enjoy the Piedmontese fare at this classic *agriturismo* restaurant, run by the regional consortium for agricultural products. It's no surpise that strictly local ingredients (honey, meats, wine) are used in a variety of hearty dishes.
☎ 011 521 78 82
✉ Piazza Emanuele Filiberto 3a 🕑 10am-2am Mon-Sat 🚌 🚃 to Porta Palazzo

Olsen (4, D2) $
Patisserie/Café
Strudels, muffins, banoffee pie (banana, toffee and cream pie) and cherry *clafoutis* (French baked-custard pastries) are baked at this down-to-earth, jam-packed lunchtime spot. Look for the cherry-topped fairy cake outside, and fill up with a €6 lunch menu.
☎ 011 436 15 73
✉ Via Sant'Agostino 4b
🕑 noon-7pm Mon-Sat
🚌 🚃 to Piazza Castello

Osteria Mezzaluna (4, B2) $$
Mediterranean
The *mezzogiorno* (southern Italy) inspires both the menu and the wine list at this breezy, casual *osteria* (wine bar with food) near Stazione Porta Susa that showcases simply prepared Mediterranean dishes at excellent prices. The décor is typically southern too, right down to the spooky Sicilian *pupa* (puppet).
☎ 011 518 52 55
✉ Via Bertola 57
🕑 noon-3pm & 7pm-1am Mon-Fri, 7pm-1am Sat 🚌 🚃 to Piazza Statuto or 🚌 🚃 🚃 to Porta Susa

Pautasso (3, D5) $$
Piedmontese
Fans of bruschetta, pizza and *bagna cauda* often crowd this convivial spot on weekends for leisurely lunches and dinners. It's reminiscent of a Tuscan farmhouse, with deep-red walls, vines and rustic details, but the food is definitely from Piedmont. Try the good-value degustation menu (€20), which includes classics such as the aforementioned *bagna cauda* (without garlic) and excellent *agnolotti* (meat-filled pasta).
☎ 011 436 67 06 ✉ Piazza Emanuele Filiberto 4 🕑 12.30-2.30pm & 8pm-1am Tue-Sun 🚌 🚃 to Porta Palazzo

San Giors (3, D5) $$$
Piedmontese
This is a charming local restaurant with a loyal and devoted following and a fantastic location near the

Pop into cheap and cheerful La Focacceria Tipica Ligure for a quick bite

Porta Palazzo markets. Any of the chicken dishes are worth trying – and you'll have no doubts about the freshness of anything coming out of the busy kitchen, thanks to said market location.

☎ 011 436 02 08 ✉ Via Borgo Dora 3 🕑 12.30-2.30pm & 8-10.30pm Tue-Sun 🚌 🚋 to Porta Palazzo

San Tommaso 10 (4, E3) $$$
Creative Piedmontese
The historic premises (see p87) flaunt a wildly unsuccessful renovation (it looks like a stand at an advertising convention), but you'll be hard-pressed to fault the food or the service at the excellent restaurant here. The market produce focuses on what's best right now, so you may come up against a long list of *carciofi* (artichoke) dishes in November, or, better yet, find enjoyable ways to sample the fabulous white truffles that will set you back €400 per kilogram (you'll only need a few grams though).

☎ 011 53 42 01 ✉ Via San Tommaso 10 🕑 noon-2.30pm & 8-10.30pm Mon-Sat 🚌 🚋 to Piazza Castello

Savoia (4, D1) $$$
Piedmontese
The smooth-as-silk Savoia presents beautifully prepared seasonal fare in style, and has a solid reputation in this fashionable quarter. We couldn't fault the *tajarin con carciofi e*

Getting Down to Business
Many of Turin's eating establishments are perfectly suited to closing the deal and doing business, but if you're really out to impress, try **Ristorante del Cambio** (p70) for old-fashioned flair, **La Pista** (p81) for incredible views, **Combal.Zero** (p72) for Michelin-starred morsels, **C'era Una Volta** (p80) for local dishes in smart surrounds, or **Al Garamond** (p68) for solid, never-a-problem service.

---

tartufo nero with *zabaione al parmigiano* (a thin pasta with artichokes, black truffles and a parmesan *zabaione* – €13), and neither could our fellow diners. Service is flawless, if a tad frosty at times, and the wine list excellent. A choice of set menus covers a number of bases, including vegetarian.

☎ 011 436 22 88 ✉ Via Corte d'Appello 13 🕑 noon-2pm & 8-10pm Mon-Fri, 8-10pm Sat 🚌 52, 60

Seiperotto (4, D1) $$$
Piedmontese
Seiperotto bills itself as an art/food/drink kind of place and certainly lives up to its claims. It's not a bad spot to pop in for an early evening drink (they'll even serve you Swedish *glögg* – mulled wine – if you're *that* cold), but a look at the menu reveals quite a few tasty morsels, such as *cinghiale* (boar). Rotating art shows line the pale green walls throughout the year too.

☎ 011 433 87 38 ✉ Via delle Orfane 17 🕑 6pm-2am Mon-Fri, 6pm-3am Sat & Sun 🚌 52, 60

Sicomoro (4, D2) $$$
Piedmontese
Utilising an old building in the heart of the city to showcase a sexy refurbishment, the team at Sicomoro know how to impress, and as a result this place gets very crowded very quickly. The menu generally features simple local dishes (*salsiccia con piselli* – sausage with peas to you and me) expertly prepared, and the Sunday brunch is definitely worth making a reservation for.

☎ 011 440 72 46 ✉ Via Stampatori 6 🕑 12.30-2.30pm & 7pm-12.30am Sun, 12.15-2.30pm & 7.30pm-12.30am Tue-Fri, 7.30pm-12.30am Mon & Sat 🚌 🚋 to Piazza Solferino or Piazza Castello

Trattoria Spirito Santo (4, E2) $$
Mediterranean
You'll find yourself on the receiving end of one of Turin's warmest welcomes at this simple, small trattoria, where the menu consists of Southern Italian–style 'surf and turf'. Take your pick of what appeals (the pasta with *bottarga di tonno* – tuna roe – will transport you to Sicily if you're having a case

of the blahs) and relax –
you're among friends.
☎ 011 436 08 77
✉ Largo IV Marzo 11
🕙 noon-3pm & 7pm-
1am Tue-Sun 🚌 🚊 to
Via XX Settembre

Trattoria Valenza (3, D5) $$
Piedmontese
Something of a ritual for
nearby market goers, pop-
ping into this simply fur-
nished, family-run trattoria
often involves eating more
than you intended to (any
of the roasts are great, and
there's a fair smattering of
offal too), getting dragged
into a boisterous family row
about who-knows-what
and losing all sense of time
in a joint that time forgot.
Fabulous stuff.
☎ 011 521 39 14 ✉ Via
Borgo Dora 39 🕙 noon-
3pm & 8-10pm Mon-Sat
🚌 🚊 to Porta Palazzo

Tre Galline (4, E1) $$$
Piedmontese
A former haunt of writer
Cesare Pavese, this much-
loved trompe l'oeil–
decorated restaurant is
a stone's throw from the
raucous Porta Palazzo
market but exudes a
charming, relaxed calm.
Business types, families
and lovers come here to
feast on fabulous *bollito
misto* (with a range of ac-
companying sauces – €20)
or the bargain *piatto unico*
(€10) at lunch, all with
a great wine selection.
There's also a child-friendly
meal available for €10 if
you're looking to feed the
small ones.
☎ 011 436 65 53
🖥 www.3galline.it,

Italian only ✉ Via
Bellezia 37d 🕙 7.45-
11pm Mon, 12.30-2pm
& 7.45-11pm Tue-Sat
🚌 🚊 to Porta
Palazzo

Volver (4, D2) $$$
Argentinian
Make a massive deposit
in your body's iron bank
with a fabulously succulent
steak from this Argentin-
ian restaurant, which also
doubles as a cultural centre
of sorts, with tango lessons
and language courses
offered. The cheerful and
colourful décor adds to its
way-south-of-the-border
appeal.
☎ 011 566 05 24
✉ Via Botero 7c
🕙 7.30pm-12.30am
Tue-Sun 🚌 🚊 to
Piazza Solferino or Piazza
Castello

Don't be chicken; if you want Piedmontese cuisine, Tre Galline is your place

PIAZZA CASTELLO TO THE PO

The streets that run off either side of Via Po are crammed with restaurants, cafés and bars that cater to the nearby university's ravenous population of students and staff, but also to many of the city's more discerning foodies.

Alla Mole (4, G3) $
Italian
This is the sort of place you stumble upon because the mood takes you to see what's going on behind the curtains. And your curiosity is rewarded in terms of atmosphere – it's a low-key, sweet place with inexpensive pasta and pizza (the *penne all'amatriciana* really hits the spot), bullfighting posters and the kind of friendly customers who courteously greet all and sundry as they enter and exit. Warm and welcoming.
☎ 011 817 47 60
✉ Via Giuseppe Verdi 10 ⏲ 12.30-3pm & 7.30pm-midnight Mon, Wed-Fri, 7.30pm-midnight Sat & Sun 🚌 🚃 to Via Po

Changing Plates
Lunch is often the most important meal of the day in Turin, and many restaurants will offer either a *menu del giorno* (menu of the day) or *piatto unico* (single plate) at lunch. The former will generally comprise a first and second course, maybe dessert and a 25cL jug of house wine or 50cL bottle of mineral water for a fixed price, while the latter will feature two courses and a vegetable side dish on the one plate for a low fixed price.

Mare Nostrum (3, E7) $$$
Seafood
Ask any local where you'll get the best fish and they'll invariably name this place. Appropriately enough, you'll find it on a street meaning 'fisherman'. Mare Nostrum is an upmarket lip-licking choice, which uses only the freshest of ingredients in its carefully thought-out menu and is a wonderful place to find the sort of Piscean delights that you might usually expect from the *mezzogiorno* (the wine list will match this). The mixed grill is, quite simply, superb.
☎ 011 839 45 43 ✉ Via Matteo Pescatore 16 ⏲ 8-10.30pm Mon-Sat 🚌 🚃 to Piazza Vittorio Veneto

Porto di Savona (4, H5) $$
Piedmontese
A lovely authentic trattoria, this laid-back eatery serves refreshingly large portions of classic Piedmontese dishes. Staples include risotto, sausage with polenta and gooey chocolate pudding. The bread sticks are also delicious. A different speciality is served each day of the week.
☎ 011 817 35 00
✉ Piazza Vittorio Veneto 2 ⏲ noon-2.30pm & 8-10.30pm Tue-Sun 🚌 🚃 to Piazza Vittorio Veneto

Nothing fishy at Mare Nostrum, yet

The real deal – Porto di Savona

Sotto La Mole (4, H4) $$$
Piedmontese
Even with the most basic Italian language skills you'll soon figure out where this place is. Smack-bang under La Mole and serving quite inventive takes on Piedmontese fare, it's an excellent place to try rich offal dishes and magnificent French-influenced sauces. Service is sterling, and certainly adds to the appeal, so expect this and the location to make it likely that you won't be the only ones wanting to eat 'sotto la Mole'.
☎ 011 817 93 98
✉ Via Montebello 9 🕒 12.30-2pm & 7.45-11pm Thu-Tue 🚌 🚃 to Via Po

LA CITTADELLA

Tiny La Cittadella is a low-key destination well away from many of the touristed areas of the city – you can dine in places that are modest and unassuming to some of the most resolutely fashionable and popular restaurants in town.

Antiche Sere $$$
Piedmontese
Book a table for this wonderful, homely restaurant that does Piedmontese fare like no other place in the city – as the saying goes, 'If it ain't broke, don't fix it' – and the fine menu here rarely changes. You'll be surrounded by locals and more meat dishes than your cardiologist would think healthy, but this is not the place to plan for clear arteries. Try the *tajarin* to start, move on to any of the wonderful pork dishes, then wallow in a superb *zabaione*.
☎ 011 385 43 47 ✉ Via Cenischia 9 🕒 8-10pm Mon-Sat 🚌 taxi

Casa Vicina (3, C8) $$$$
Piedmontese
The Vicina family has been in this caper for over 100 years, so you can rest easy that they know what they're doing in this modern space that features classic local fare (the pigs' trotters are marvellous), a great local wine list and see-through Philippe Starck seating. Reservations essential.
☎ 011 59 09 49 ✉ Via Massena 66 🕒 noon-2pm & 7.30-10.30pm Tue-Sat, noon-2pm Sun 🚃 4, 16

L'Ostú (3, A8) $
Piedmontese
With a slot machine and straight-up décor, you're not choosing this place for fine dining – but you will eat very well and cheaply (and there's a good wine list). Snaffle a plate of *tripa con fagioli* (tripe with beans) if you want to look local, or a panino stuffed with *vitello tonnato* if you're on the run. Either way, you'll be left with more money to spend

at the nearby La Crocetta markets (p55).
☎ 011 59 67 98 ⊠ Via Colombo 63 ⏱ noon-2.30pm & 8-11.30pm Mon-Sat 🚌 10, 12, 58, 58/

Shri Ganesh (3, B8) $$
Indian
Shri Ganesh is the best Indian restaurant in the city according to its many local fans, so if you're hankering for *pakora*, korma and the like you should come here. The atmosphere is friendly and easy-going, and the dishes make a nice change from a steady diet of beef,

veal and pork (easy to get stuck on in Turin).
☎ 011 59 56 80 ⊠ Via Pigafetta 14 ⏱ noon-3pm & 7.30pm-midnight Tue-Sun 🚌 10, 12, 58, 58/

Spazio (3, A8) $$$
Mediterranean
Stylish Spazio enables you to break off from an afternoon's contemplation of contemporary art and tend to your stomach's rumblings with panache. The mod-Med cuisine attracts plenty of the city's most discerning art buffs – try the *petto d'anatra con*

miele di castagno (duck breast with chestnut honey). If you're only after something quick and light, the ground-floor **café** (⏱ 11am-7pm Tue-Wed & Fri-Sun, 11am-11pm Thu) is a good choice – with pasta and salads dominating the list and Warhol-style silver couches offering respite.
☎ 011 198 316 26 ⊠ Fondazione Sandretto Re Rebaudengo, Via Modane 20a ⏱ 12.30-2.30pm & 8.30-10.30pm Tue-Sat, 12.30-3.30pm Sun 🚌 58, 58/

SAN SALVARIO & AROUND

San Salvario has become something of a pizza ghetto in the last few years, but it's also an excellent neighbourhood for newer restaurants, and is possessed of a vibrant multicultural feeling.

C'era Una Volta (5, B1) $$$
Piedmontese
Discerning business types make contact with this avowedly local restaurant (who's name translates as 'Once Upon a Time') – located on the 2nd floor of a grand townhouse – via an intercom and then revel in the classic Piedmontese fare on offer. On Friday (or by reservation) the *fritto misto* (mixed fry) proves extremely popular and filling, but if you think you can find room for the *degustazione* menu (at a very reasonable €25) it's worth an attempt.
☎ 011 65 54 98 ⊠ Corso Vittorio Emanuele II 41 ⏱ 8-11pm Mon-Sat 🚌 🚇 🚊 to Porta Nuova

Dai Saletta (3, C8) $$
Piedmontese
A hugely popular trattoria that seems to have materialised from central casting (right down to the checked tablecloths and charming management), Dai Saletta is a modest family-run place that takes considerable (and justified) pride in its cooking. The menu offers regional classics such as *brasato al Barolo* (mouth-melting tender beef braised in Barolo wine), while the wine list is dominated by Piedmontese reds. A great place to sample excellent value-for-money local cuisine, but book ahead.
☎ 011 668 78 67 ⊠ Via Belfiore 37 ⏱ 12.30-2pm & 8-10pm Mon-Sat 🚊 16, 18

Il Cubico (3, C9) $$$
Modern Piedmontese
Chef Antonio Giovanniti works wonders with market produce to create imaginative, attractive cuisine (the ravioli dishes are particularly impressive). The restaurant itself is modern but warm, and located in the 'next big thing' neighbourhood of San Salvario. Reservations advised.
☎ 011 1971 45 46 ⊠ Via Saluzzo 86bis ⏱ 12.30-2.30pm & 7.30-11pm Mon-Sat 🚌 1, 34, 35

Il Rospetto (5, B2) $
Pizzeria
Our favourite pizzas in Turin come from this place, which means 'the baby toad' in Italian. And there's nothing remotely toady about them – they are beautiful

thin-crusted delights that invite you to have another one for dessert. Only trouble is, it's a tight squeeze and the world and his wife seems to want a piece (or should that be slice?) of the action in this increasingly cool neighbourhood. Get ready to join a queue.

☎ 011 669 82 21 ✉ Piazza Madama Cristina

5 ⏱ 7.30pm-midnight Tue-Sun 🚌 to Piazza Madama Cristina

L'Idrovolante (5, C3) $$$
Italian
A stone's throw from the River Po, the Borgo Medioevale and the Parco del Valentino, this is a popular, ivy-covered spot with a reputation for romance and live music and DJ-spun sounds in the evening. It definitely comes into its own during summer Sundays, when it seems that most of the city feels the need to flock to the riverside.

☎ 011 668 76 02 ✉ Viale Virgilio 105 ⏱ 12.15-3pm & 8.15-11.30pm Tue-Sun 🚌 🚊 9, 16

LINGOTTO

This revamped FIAT factory boasts a number of simple eateries in its shopping centre (unreviewed, but all open till midnight daily) and a few grander places suited to business travellers and gourmands.

Art + Café (6, B4) $$$
Creative Mediterranean
Chef Daniele Giolitto has quite a task on his hands – how to present the sort of food that will compete with this monumental Renzo Piano–designed space. Fortunately, he does it with aplomb. That said, you'll spend a great deal of your time here oohing and aahing over the blood-red chairs, the cherry-wood panelling and the vast, airy dimensions of the whole shebang.

☎ 011 664 28 20 ✉ Via Nizza 230 ⏱ 24hr (hotel guests) 🚌 1, 35 🚊 18

La Pista (6, A4) $$$$
Modern Piedmontese
An ultra-stylish combination of industrial chic, understated luxury and wonderful mountain views, La Pista exudes a 'restaurant of the moment' vibe and is an excellent spot for a smart business lunch or dinner. Overlooking the legendary race track on the roof of the Lingotto Fiere, its location is as memorable as the food. New takes on Piedmont classics are the hallmark of chef Massimo Guzzone's beautifully presented dishes. Advance booking is essential.

☎ 011 631 35 23 ✉ Via Nizza 262 ⏱ 12.30-3pm & 7.30-11pm Wed-Mon 🚌 1, 35 🚊 18

Torpedo (6, A4) $$$$
Creative Mediterranean
If you don't feel as though you've had your fill of green scenes whilst in Turin, then you should hightail it here, where the outlook over a lush, verdant internal garden serves as an unexpected escape from the city streets. Fabulously inventive dishes combine traditional flavours with stunning presentation and automotive fans get to drool over the original Torpedo car on the premises, as well as the food.

☎ 011 664 27 14 ✉ Via Nizza 262 ⏱ 24hr (hotel guests) 🚌 1, 35 🚊 18

Self-Catering Options
Cream of the crop for self-caterers is obviously the expansive Porta Palazzo Market (p12), but Turin is also crammed with some delightful speciality shops stocking food and wine (p66). If it's a supermarket that you're after, try **Di per Di** (4, C1; Piazza Savoia 2; ⏱ 8.30am-7.30pm Mon, Tue & Thu-Sat, 8.30am-noon Wed), which is part of a city-wide chain and has fairly well-stocked delicatessen counters and often fresh bread.

OVER THE PO

Not too many tourists end up crossing the river to eat, but plenty of locals do – and with good reason. Here are some of our faves.

Con Calma $$$
Piedmontese
Fans of *finanziera* (a combination of chicken livers and sweetbreads) will be in heaven at this delightfully welcoming, cosy restaurant near Superga. Great care is taken with all the dishes, and the wine list is avowedly local, meaning that this place gets packed with regulars and clued-up visitors. Reservations are a good idea.
☎ 011 898 02 29
✉ Strada Comunale del Cartman 59 ☾ 8-11pm Tue-Sat, 1-2.30pm & 8-11pm Sun 🚗 taxi

I Birilli $$$
Creative Piedmontese
Frequented by actors and football players and owned by a local celeb, the comic Piero Chiambretti, this is a wildly popular over-the-Po restaurant, with a great mix of traditional and modern cuisine and rather large portions. A member of *Le Tavole di Sapore* (Tables of Taste), an organisation set up by the city tourist authority, it offers a good-value set menu at lunch and dinner.
☎ 011 819 05 67
✉ Strada Val San Martino 6 ☾ 12.30-2.30pm & 7.30-10.30pm 🚌 54 🚗 taxi

La Cantinella (3, E7) $$$
Italian
La Cantinella is a very popular local restaurant (reservations are a good idea)

that seems to cater to just about every demographic. There are 'mega salads' for vegetarians, children are more than welcome, and for some reason, a lot of people seem to end up dancing to the Macarena on tables when enough wine has been imbibed.
☎ 011 819 33 11
✉ Corso Moncalieri 3a ☾ 7.30pm-1am 🚌 to Piazza Vittorio Veneto or Piazza Gran Madre di Dio

Restaurante Revolución $$
Mexican
A funky, colourful place where few tourists find themselves and offering plenty of bean-fuelled excuses to guzzle tequila while you eat. Not confining its appeal solely to the

flatulent or inebriated, this place is also a good spot for vegetarians and kids (there's a menu for the little ones that goes easy on the chilli).
☎ 011 890 00 73
✉ Corso Casale 194b ☾ 7pm-1.30am Wed-Mon 🚌 61

Stazione Sassi $$
Pizzeria
This is a dandy, handy choice for those experiencing hunger pains before or after a trip to Basilica di Superga. It's spacious and serves both light café fare and more substantial Italian dishes, including good pizzas.
☎ 011 899 75 13
✉ Piazzale Modena 6 ☾ 7pm-midnight Tue-Sat, noon-3pm & 7pm-midnight Sun 🚊 15

Entertainment

Turin, that most industrious and disciplined of Italy's cities, doesn't mind socialising at some of its famous cafés during the day, but really lets loose after dark, and preparations for the night ahead begin in earnest with cocktail hour (about 7pm), when the city's bartenders mix potent drinks or *aperitivi*, lay on sumptuous (and gratis) spreads of *stuzzichini* (snacks) and wait for the young and old to flood the bars with gossip, chat and flirtation. All this can serve as pre-dinner prep or a pre-clubbing warm-up.

Clubbing in Turin is taken seriously – with dozens of late-night options that will have you wishing you'd packed more plasters for dance-happy feet. The main clubbing districts are Murazzi, the riverside strip of dance clubs that lines the Po, and Docks Dora (3, D3), the former industrial zone filled with edgy outlets. Don't expect things to start going off until about 1am though. Electronica is immensely popular here, and there are numerous talented DJs, producers and musicians on the scene creating beats and blends. If rock and roll or pop is more your thing – you'll find venues catering for that too.

Cinemas and theatres abound in Turin, with knowledgeable film and theatre crowds eager to see the latest and greatest productions (cinemas are especially packed on weekends). Concert halls echo to the sounds of classical orchestras, world-famous soloists and the more experimental end of things. Classical ballet and very good contemporary dance can also be enjoyed at a range of performance spaces, with the prosaic choreography of football performed by two very famous teams indeed – Juventus and Torino.

See p114 for bus or tram numbers to the routes listed in this chapter.

Ticketing

Tickets for rock and other mainstream concerts are sold at **FNAC** (4, E3; ☎ 011 551 67 11; Via Roma 56; ☽ 9.30am-8pm Mon-Sat 10am-8pm Sun) and **Ricordi Media Store** (4, E5; ☎ 011 562 11 56; Piazza CLN 251; ☽ 9am-7.30pm Mon-Sat, 10am-1pm & 3.30-7.30pm Sun). **Vetrina per Torino** (4, C4; ☎ 011 506 99 67; www.torinocultura.it,; Atrium Torino; ☽ 9.30am-7pm Mon-Sat, 11am-7pm Sun) has cultural information and a ticketing service.

Listings

Entertainment listings are included in *Torino Sette*, the insert of newspaper *La Stampa*; cinema, theatre and exhibition listings are also included in its daily *Spettacoli Cronaca* section. Also worth picking up at the tourist office and in many bars is the free 80-page *News Spettacolo* (www.newspettacolo.com, Italian only), a weekly booklet listing several hundred entertainment venues, ranging from straight to gay to innocent to downright dirty. Many venues have their own websites listing upcoming events.

CAFÉS

Partly due to Turin's legacy of French and Austrian involvement, the city has a flourishing café scene. Many of the historic cafés date from the 19th century, when Risorgimento heroes, intellectuals and town gadabouts would flock to their ornate bars. We can't think of a better city for a sinfully rich hot chocolate in elaborate surrounds…

Al Bicerin (3, C5)
We wouldn't lie to you, we based ourselves close to this piazza so we could come here as often as possible, much like Cavour and Dumas, who were also fans of the fabulous *bicerin* (a sublime Turinese blend of coffee, hot chocolate, milk and whipped cream) that gave this place its name. Going strong since 1763, and still run exclusively by women, it's a tiny gem of a place, located at the foot of a 14th-century bell tower that looms over one

Special Events

January *Linguaggi Jazz* (www.centrojazztorino.it, Italian only) – Runs to April and makes the whole city swing, with concerts and themed films.

February *Automotoretrò* (www.automotoretro.it, Italian only) – Classic cars at – where else? – the Lingotto Fiere.

March *International Women's Cinema Festival* – Eight days of films, shorts and documentaries by, with and for women, and coinciding with International Women's Day (8 March).

April *Big Torino* (www.bigtorino.net) – Biennial of emerging art provides a showcase for young artists. The next is due in 2006.
Turin International Gay & Lesbian Film Festival (www.turinglfilmfestival.com) – Going strong for over 20 years and with the catchiest catchphrase in town, 'Da Sodoma a Hollywood'.
Turin Marathon (www.turinmarathon.it) – Forty-two kilometres of Turin (the half-marathon takes place in September).

May *Fiera del Libro* (www.fieralibro.it) – Enormous book fair with all the publishing houses and some big names in literature at Lingotto Fiere.
Interplay (www.juvarramultiteatro.it, Italian only or www.mosaicodanza.it) – Fabulous experimental dance fest held at the end of May in Teatro Juvarra.

June *Chicobum* (www.barrumba.com/chicobum/, Italian only) – From June to the end of July local and international mainstream pop, dance and rock acts play in the nearby area of Borgaro. Scrounge a lift or drive.
Festività di San Giovanni Battista – On 24 June Turin celebrates the feast of its patron – St John the Baptist. Expect festivities to fill the streets.
Momenti Estate – Street events such as concerts, dances and processions on the banks of the mighty Po – until September.

of the city's most charming piazzas.

☎ 011 436 93 25
✉ **Piazza della Consolata 5** ⊙ 8.30am-7.30pm Mon, Tue, Thu & Fri, 8.30am-1pm & 3.30-7.30pm Sat & Sun 🚌 52, 60

Baratti & Milano (4, F3)
Situated at the entrance to the Galleria Subalpina, Baratti & Milano has been serving coffee, cakes and light lunches since 1873. Crowds flock here on

Sunday to buy cakes, sweets and biscuits (boxed and ribbon-wrapped) from its old-fashioned shop counter. The lunchtime *piatto unico* (€16) is a reasonable deal, although the atmosphere is a tad 'God's waiting room'.

☎ 011 561 30 60
✉ **Piazza Castello 27** ⊙ 8am-9pm Tue-Sun 🚌 🚋 to Piazza Castello

Bar Barolino Cocchi (4, D1)
There are worse ways to start your day than with

a sublime cappuccino and newspaper at this delightful establishment. Housed in a Juvarra-designed building, its petite dimensions don't preclude it from having its own dome, and more presence than some of the gilt-trippin' gin palaces at the posher end of town.

☎ 011 436 72 45
✉ **Via Bonelli 16c** ⊙ 8am-8pm Mon-Sat 🚌 🚋 to **Porta Palazzo**

July *Torino Free Festival* (www.trafficfestival.com, Italian only) – Three days of big local and international names like (in recent times) Iggy Pop, Lou Reed, Felix Da Housecat, Subsonica, Mau Mau, Africa Unite and others.

September *Torino Settembre Musica* (www.comune.torino.it/settembremusica/, Italian only) – Two concerts of classical and contemporary music daily for 36 days.
Contrappunti (www.mosaicodanza.it) – Modern dance and other art forms combine, with an emphasis on unusual locations.

October *Blues al Femminile* (www.centrojazztorino.it/blues.html, Italian only) – Performances by female blues artists until December. Organised by Centro Jazz Torino.
Cinemambiente (www.cinemambiente.it) – A film festival devoted to environmental themes.
Musica 90 (www.musica90.net, Italian only) – A world music festival that extends from the end of October to mid-December with jazz, pop and world all represented at Lingotto Fiere.
Salone del Gusto (www.slowfood.it, Italian only) – If food is the new porn, this is where the orgy happens. Thousands of stalls, gourmands and much lip-licking at this biennial event'.

November *Artissima* (www.artissima.it) – Modern and contemporary art trade fair at Lingotto Fiere and galleries throughout town.
Club to Club (www.clubtoclub.it, Italian only) – Turin throbs to pulsing beats with this international electronica festival.
Luci d'Artista (www.torinoartecontemporanea.it) – Reason enough for coming – Turin's streets are illuminated with contemporary art as local and international artists create one-off wonders for various public spaces.
Sottodiciotto Film Festival (www.aiacetorino.it, Italian only) – Films for the under 18s by the under 18s. Going strong for over 18 years.
Turin Film Festival (www.torinofilmfest.org) – Prestigious but unpretentious film fest with international and local names.

Al Bicerin (p84) – where chocolate, coffee and whipped cream share a cup

Caffè Mulassano (4, F3)
An Art-Nouveau gem (built 1907–09) lined with a marble floor, mirrored walls, a coffered ceiling and even four tables (no mean feat considering the size of the place). As in days gone by, the theatre mob from nearby Teatro Regio (p94) adores this relic. It was here that the *tramezzino* (small sandwich) was invented. Try some, and have an *aperitivo Mulassano* (€4.65).
☎ 011 54 79 90
✉ Piazza Castello 15
🕑 7.30am-10.30pm
🚌 🚊 to Piazza Castello

Caffé San Carlo (4, E4)
The San Carlo's last radical innovation appears to have been the installation of gas lighting in the 19th century. Other than that, it seems remarkably unchanged since 1822, and has attracted Risorgimento nationalists, business-suited captains of industry and well-heeled tourists for many years, whilst offering white-jacketed service and 28 different types of coffee. Just edged out in the lavish stakes by the nearby Torino, simply because of size.
☎ 011 53 25 86
✉ Piazza San Carlo 156 🕑 8am-1am
🚌 🚊 🚊 to Porta Nuova or Piazza Castello

Caffé Torino (4, E4)
Heavy brocade, chandeliers, tinsel-bedecked sweets, a spiral staircase and fur-clad ladies all come together to make this one of the most sumptuous cafés in town.

Brown Sugar
For true chocoholics who have trawled the city's streets popping into speciality stores and famous cafés, nothing can beat **CioccolaTò,** the city's grand homage to chocolate. A three-week festival that begins in late February, its opening fair in Piazza Castello draws huge crowds who flock to taste, point, nibble and marvel at the huge array of chocolate curiosities on display.

A city-wide initiative, it encompasses chocolate workshops, sculptures and films while many restaurants participate by offering chocolate-based menus. To save a few euros (if not a few kilos), buy a special chocopass (€10), which pays for 10 tastings in a 24-hour period. For more information, check out www.cioccola-to.com (in Italian).

And did we mention the superb hot chocolate? If it's too hot for all that, a freshly squeezed orange juice will hit the spot, particularly if you're sitting down and haven't yet read the bill. The frescoed ceiling has it right when it says: 'A little too much is just enough for me'. When you're leaving, be sure to rub your shoe across the brass bull in the pavement for good luck.
☎ 011 54 51 18
✉ Piazza San Carlo 204 ⏱ 7.30am-1am
🚌 🚋 🚊 to Porta Nuova or Piazza Castello

Neuv Caval 'd Brôns (4, E4)

With a lavish, vaulted trompe l'oeil ceiling, this place doubles as a sophisticated café and a purveyor of tasty little cakes and delicate pastries that are so minutely exquisite you can cram them in and still look ladylike. We hope.
☎ 011 54 53 54
✉ Piazza San Carlo 157 ⏱ 8am-9pm Thu-Tue
🚌 🚋 🚊 to Porta Nuova or Piazza Castello

Norman (4, D3)

On the fringes of the *centro storico* (historic centre), this chandelier-lit café is a good bet for a lunchtime plate of pasta (from €5). In summer, tables spill out beneath the arcade and the city's attractive and well-dressed middle class flocks to see and be seen, day or night.
☎ 011 54 08 54
✉ Via Pietro Micca 22 ⏱ 8am-1am 🚌 to Piazza Solferino

Lavazza Lovers

Coffee connoisseurs crowd the narrow bar at **San Tommaso 10** (4, E3), mulling over a menu that includes orange cappuccino and tiramisu espresso. The cappuccino, which tastes like the most natural combination in the world, is a winner. Luigi Lavazza, father of the eponymous coffee brand, first began roasting beans here in the 1890s. See p68 for a review of the mod-Italian restaurant on the premises.

Platti (4, B6)

The favourite café of author Cesare Pavese and editor Giulio Einaudi, the original interior (built in 1870), a riot of old-world charm, remains intact at this sweet-laden coffee, cake and liquor shop. Skip the noisy terrace and lunch beneath gold leaf inside, where a very tempting buffet masquerades as the *menu del giorno* (€15.50) and service is admirably considerate.
☎ 011 506 90 56 ✉ Corso Vittorio Emanuele II 72 ⏱ 7.30am-9pm
🚌 🚋 🚊 to Porta Nuova

BARS

Turin's dozens of bars range from the steadfastly local to the fashionably ethnic, the traditional to the out-there, but you can bet you'll get not only a good stiff drink when you want one, but also a choice of tempting titbits in this most civilised Italian city.

Café 21 (4, J6)

Now that *absinthe* is the drink to be seen drinking (until you're having trouble seeing straight), you may as well be seen drinking it somewhere special – and 21 is just such a place. A stellar location, lush decorative touches and a crowd that does louche with style.
☎ 011 812 22 09
✉ Piazza Vittorio Veneto 21 🕒 7pm-2am Tue-Sun 🚌 🚋 to Piazza Vittorio Veneto

Caffè Elena (4, J5)

This is one of our favourites, as it combines a sense of history (Nietzsche was a regular) with a good amount of modern panache (Philippe Starck chairs). Peruse the list of cocktails, wines or the grappa selection amidst the blood-red walls of the main salon, then amble over to the groaning snack table and pick a morsel or two. The bathroom, a little off the premises, is surprisingly space age.
☎ 011 812 33 41 ✉ Piazza Vittorio Veneto 5 🕒 8.30am-midnight Mon,

Tue, Thu & Sun, 8.30am-1am Fri & Sat 🚌 🚋 to Piazza Vittorio Veneto

Caffè Flora (4, J6)

A pre-dinner cocktail (or a Punt e Mes – see the box) slips down a treat at this Po-side café with plump comfy chairs. Alternatively, come a little earlier to pass some time with an English newspaper, waiting for the early evening nibbles to make an appearance. Not in the least trendy or posh – just easy-peasy.
☎ 011 817 15 30
✉ Piazza Vittorio Veneto 24 🕒 2pm-3am Tue-Fri, noon-3am Sat & Sun 🚌 🚋 to Piazza Vittorio Veneto

Ciak Bar (4, H4)

With a subterranean ambience, film-related themed events and live jazz, it's no wonder this place is so popular. Located in the Mole Antonelliana (p8), it is particularly popular on Saturdays after a visit to the Museo Nazionale del Cinema.
☎ 335 61 42 103
✉ Via Montebello 20

🕒 9am-8pm Sun, Tue-Fri, 9am-11pm Sat 🚌 🚋 to Via Po

Damadama Café (5, B2)

Spread over three floors, there's something really cool going on here – provided you like wine, music and tapas, that is. The building itself is quite labyrinthine, with different rooms offering quite varied options – right down to second-hand CD sales. The overall feeling is relaxed, unhurried and a little Middle Eastern.
☎ 011 65 57 11 ✉ Piazza Madama Cristina 6 🕒 6pm-1am Tue-Sat, noon-1am Sun 🚌 to Piazza Madama Cristina

Dual (4, F4)

Dual is so subtly posh-looking that you might dismiss it as out of your league, which would be a mistake. It's a very handy spot that covers a number of bases, and proffers mean cocktails to well-dressed patrons. What got us excited was that it also caters to those who like a big breakfast or brunch the morning after the night before. Eat, drink and be merry – as long as you don't look so merry you spoil the illusion of being unflappable.
☎ 011 812 84 36
✉ Piazza Carlo Alberto 17d 🕒 8am-2am 🚌 🚋 to Piazza Castello

Make a Point of It...

One *aperitivo* (aperitif) you simply must try is the local creation **Punt e Mes**, which was first made in 1870 and is a refreshingly bitter version of that old standby vermouth.

Fish (3, C5)

Check out the Dali-inspired living room as you enter. A laid-back brick vault of a place with very dim lights, you can enjoy a late dinner or, on Thursday to Saturday nights, the cool DJ-spun music. An excellent spot, and a likely highlight of a night in the Quadrilatero Romano if you're venturing out with a small group of friends.

☎ 011 521 79 33 ✉ Via Valerio 5b 🕑 7pm-3am Tue-Sun 🚌 52, 60

Frog (4, D3)

The Frog is a good-sized bar and entertainment venue with an emphasis on hip hop and R&B when the weekend hits. It's quiet early in the evening, but gets pretty crowded after midnight. The décor is warm and inviting, but not flash.

☎ 011 440 77 36 ✉ Via dei Mercanti 19 🕑 7pm-3am Tue-Sun 🚌 🚊 to Piazza Castello

Gran Bar (3, E7)

Gran Bar, over the Po, is stylish, modern and an excellent spot to sample local tipples, as it has regular wine tasting sessions. Service is friendly and lets you sit at your table, lazy-boy style. Easily the most fashionable spot in this quarter, and worth crossing the river for.

☎ 011 813 08 71 ✉ Piazza Gran Madre di Dio 2 🕑 7am-2am 🚌 🚊 to Piazza Gran Madre di Dio or Piazza Vittorio Veneto

Hafa Café (4, D1)

Its nomenclature is a homage to the notorious Hafa Café in Tangier, Morocco,

---

The Other Face of Piedmont

Gianduja is not just a hazelnut chocolate paste to die for. It is a stock character in the 16th-century comedy, *Commedia dell'Arte*, and in the late 18th century Turinese puppeteer Gian Battista Sales turned the cheery chap into a marionette. Today, it's the face of Piedmont – albeit in the shape of a mask – at carnival.

Conservative, good humoured, naive and honest are characteristics embodied by Gianduja, the Piedmontese puppet peasant, whose original name in local dialect was Giöan d'la douja (*douja* being a terracotta wine jug unique to Asti in regional Piedmont). The plucky little fellow has three big loves in life – food, wine and his girlfriend Giacometta. Recognise him by his red-trimmed brown jacket, yellow waistcoat, pea-green knickerbockers and tomato-red stockings.

Springtime carnival aside, Gianduja appears at the traditional celebrations held in Turin on 24 June to honour San Giovanni (St John), the city's patron saint.

---

and while you won't find the likes of Paul Bowles and William Burroughs smoking *kif* on the premises, you will find a magic lantern–strewn interior and a delightful spot to sip mint tea, enjoy a glass of Moroccan wine or graze on the spicy couscous. The charming service and an attached homewares/gift shop will most likely see you popping in regularly if you find yourself in this part of town.

☎ 011 436 70 91 ✉ Via Sant'Agostino 23c 🕑 11am-2am

Tue-Sat, 6.30pm-1am Sun 🚌 🚊 to Porta Palazzo

KM5 (4, D1)

First impressions will give you the idea that this is a small 'local' with a good range of drinks, but feel free to wander around and find the comfy rooms with ample seating that let you curl up, stretch out and socialise with abandon. Very good music is played – from reggae to pop and electronica.

☎ 011 431 00 32 ✉ Via San Domenico

14/16 ☯ 6pm-3am Tue-Sat 🚌 🚇 to Porta Palazzo

La Drogheria (4, J5)

This bar sports a laidback sensibility that ably assists the university crowd's attempts to ease into the night. There are comfy plump sofas, simple eating options and some very decently priced drinks on offer. An easygoing, cheery vibe predominates and it's not a bad place at all to recuperate from a hangover either.

☎ 011 812 24 14 ✉ Piazza Vittorio Veneto 18 ☯ 11am-2am 🚌 🚇 to Piazza Vittorio Veneto

Lobelix (4, C1)

The terrace on Piazza Savoia is a favourite with the in crowd for eye-crossingly potent *aperitivi* (aperitifs; €7); its banquet of snacks laid out from 7pm is one of Turin's most extravagant, and the in crowd are prepared to come out of their shells and chat. In winter, there's a cosy, low-lit vibe spread out over two floors.

☎ 011 436 72 06 ✉ Via Corte d'Appello 15f ☯ 7pm-3am Mon-Sat 🚌 52, 60

Pastis (3, D5)

Pastis is a great spot to linger over a drink at any time of the day or night, especially when it's warm and you've nabbed a table in the piazza. The crowd here is comprised of local bohemian types and young artists, while the décor is showing its age. Not too

cool and not too hot – just right.

☎ 011 521 10 85 ✉ Piazza Emanuele Filiberto 9 ☯ 9am-3.30pm & 6pm-2am 🚌 🚇 to Porta Palazzo

Shore (3, D5)

If they had alcohol on the Gucci catwalk this is what it would look like. So fashionable it's almost painful (this place was certainly one of the in-crowd's haunts when we visited), but definitely worth a visit for the super cocktails and the chance to catch sight of yourself in the very flattering lighting. The music ranges from unobtrusive house to cruisey jazz, and service is smooth as silk.

☎ 011 436 34 96 ✉ Piazza Emanuele Filiberto 10e ☯ 8pm-2am Tue-Sun 🚌 🚇 to Porta Palazzo

Suite 29 (5, D1)

A perennially popular 'dinner club' (without the restaurant) haunt for the city's fashionable 30-somethings, the rooms in this renovated townhouse ooze magazine-spread chic and invite studied posing on its sofas, spread out among lavish floral arrangements. Get past the door by leaving your comfy shoes at home and being prepared to look and be looked at. Good *mojitos*.

☎ 011 1971 49 02 ✉ Via della Rocca 29a ☯ 7pm-2am Tue-Thu, 7pm-3am Fri & Sat, 7pm-1am Sun 🚌 🚇 to Via Po

Taberna Libraria (4, G4)

Quite possibly the most

civilised way to imbibe in the city and boost your brain cells at the same time (a rare thing). Taberna Libraria won't get done for false advertising – it really is a wine/bookshop, and serves very good tapas to boot – meaning that you can tick a number of experiential boxes once you've walked in the door and found your spot.

☎ 011 83 65 15 ✉ Via Bogino 5b ☯ 10am-9pm 🚌 🚇 to Piazza Castello

I Tre Galli (4, D1)

With its 1000-plus wine list and some very tasty local dishes on the menu (the lunch menu is excellent value), this place is social central during the summer months, when huge crowds descend on this neighbourhood to party alfresco. Décor is stylish but unpretentious, as is the service – expect the chef to pop out in a rare quiet moment and prop up the bar if he spies a familiar face.

☎ 011 521 60 27 ✉ Via Sant'Agostino 25 ☯ noon-2.30pm & 6pm-2am Mon-Sat 🚌 🚇 to Porta Palazzo

Vinicola Al Sorij (4, J5)

A popular spot to stop, sit and sip after a hard day, this tiny place just behind Piazza Vittorio Veneto has a cellar of more than 500 different wines and some more-ish offerings for both your plate and your palate.

☎ 011 83 56 67 ✉ Via Matteo Pescatore 10c ☯ 6pm-2am Mon-Sat 🚌 🚇 to Piazza Vittorio Veneto

NIGHTCLUBS

Generally, nightclubs don't have a cover charge unless a live band is playing. Nightlife zones are often seasonal – the Murazzi is wildly popular in summer, less so in winter, when the Docks Dora and Quadrilatero Romano areas prove more attractive.

Alcatraz (5, E1)
This den of dance is a particular fave with Turin's industrial deafness sufferers, with relentless beats and basslines punishing those who can't dance to save themselves. Thank God for the long list of potent drinks that help create an illusion of not being cursed with two left feet.
☎ 011 83 69 00 ✉ Via Murazzi del Po 37 ⏰ 10pm-4am Jun-Sep, 10pm-4am Tue-Sat Oct-Dec, 10pm-4am Thu-Sat Jan-May 🚌 🚃 to Piazza Vittorio Veneto

Barrumba (4, H4)
Barrumba hosts live music acts, but its popularity is largely due to the fact that it crams in an enthusiastic, up-for-it crowd of dancers from Thursday to Saturday, when a stellar playlist might include rock, punk, pop, house, drum & bass or anything else that suits the moment. The music doesn't start until midnight as the club is under a cinema. For the young and young at heart.
☎ 011 819 43 47 ✉ Via San Massimo 1 € Friday €6 ⏰ 11pm-5am Tue & Thu-Sat 🚌 🚃 to Via Po

Beach (5, E1)
An airy, brick-steel-and-glass temple of dance embedded in the riverside docks (as close to a beach as you'll get in this city when summer hits and things move outdoors). A party-hearty, fashionably dressed crowd shakes out the cobwebs with relish and the air is thick with fun. Great DJs, great visuals and great atmosphere combine to make this a must-see on a clubbing pilgrimage. Don't bother arriving until midnight at the earliest.
☎ 011 88 87 77 💻 www.thebeachtorino

.it, Italian only ✉ Via Murazzi del Po 18-22 ⏰ 7pm-5am Tue-Sun 🚌 🚃 to Piazza Vittorio Veneto

Da Giancarlo (5, E1)
Watch a mixed crowd (dreadlocked, suited, you name it) go right off after hours, with plenty of swaying (to the music, the *fumo* (pot) and the booze) and lots of laughs. An institution of the best kind – and recommended by many as the proper way to end a real night out. Grungy, grotty and great. Be prepared to explain that you're not a member of ARCI (Associazione Ricreativa e Culturale Italiana) at the door – but flash your driving licence from home and you're fine.
☎ 011 81 74 72 ✉ Via Murazzi del Po 45 ⏰ 11pm-7am Tue-Sun 🚌 🚃 to Piazza Vittorio Veneto

Hennessy
Populist doof-doof music choices provide the soundtrack to Turin's sweaty set, who run to the hills to dance all night long during the summer months. Lots of seating for when your legs give out.
☎ 011 899 85 22 💻 www.hennessy club.com, Italian only ✉ Strada Traforo del Pino 23 € €20 ⏰ 11pm-5am Tue-Sat 🚌 taxi

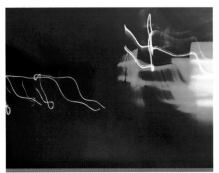
Trip the light fantastic at Alcatraz

Block Rockin' Docks

One of the biggest stars of Turin's famed nightlife is **Docks Dora** (3, D3; Via Valprato 68), a converted 1912 warehouse complex that was once an industrial zone and now plays host to some of the city's most interesting and enjoyable clubbing options. Check out the fabulously all-over-the-shop Café Blue (with its reggae, rock, punk and hip-hop offerings), Docks8 (when too much techno is never enough – even on a Sunday morning) and Docks Home (with its more arty ambience and great DJ sets). Clubs here generally operate from midnight until 6am on Friday and Saturday nights, and although technically you'll need to be a member of ARCI (Associazione Ricreativa e Culturale Italiana), you can probably get away with showing your passport or driving licence to the bouncer.

Jammin' (5, E1)

If you're here to dance, be aware things don't get started until after 1am, but in summer there are outdoor tables and a good range of cocktails to aid a segue from day to night and beyond. Jammin' is very much an Ibiza-style club –with hands in the air, dancing on podiums and skimpy fashions, plus oceans of sweat.
☎ 011 88 28 69
✉ Via Murazzi del Po 17-19 🕑 7pm-5am Apr-Oct 🚌 🚊 to Piazza Vittorio Veneto

LIVE MUSIC

Café Procope (4, A1)

Catch live blues, jazz, flamenco and independent theatre at this flexible venue. A little gem. The crowd, while enthusiastic and friendly, is more mature than at some live music venues in town – although not so old that bedtime has become an issue.
☎ 011 54 06 75
✉ Via Juvarra 15
🚌 🚊 🚉 to Porta Susa

Folk Club (4, B2)

You can bank on seeing world music, jazz and, of course, folk music at this well-regarded venue with a loyal following and strong sense of history.
☎ 011 53 76 36
🖥 www.folkclub .it, Italian only ✉ Via Perrone 3b 🕑 varies
🚌 🚊 🚉 to Porta Susa

Hiroshima Mon Amour

The fabulous HMA covers all the alternative bases, with DJs, jazz, cabaret, techno and everything in between. Big enough to feel like an occasion when you go here, small enough to feel like you belong.
☎ 011 317 66 36
🖥 www.hiroshima monamour.org, Italian

only ✉ Via Bossoli 83
€ free-€20 🕑 from 9pm 🚊 Lingotto
🚌 14, 14/, 74

Magazzino di Gilgamesh (3, A5)

Something of a musical hothouse, di Gilgamesh is a well known venue for live blues, jazz and rock, although you can also catch Latino and

With a lineup as bizarre as its name, HMA is a winner

world music here plus get a decent bite to eat lest your rumbling tum threatens to drown out the music.
☎ 011 749 28 01
🖥 www.gilgamesh torino.it, Italian only
✉ Piazza Monceniso 13b
€ varies 🚊 9, 16

Mazdapalace
This is where you'll hear big international and Italian acts, as it's Turin's premier pop arena. Not much in the way of intimacy, but acoustics seem to be pretty good for this kind of venue.
☎ 011 455 90 90
🖥 www.mazdapalace.it,

Italian only ✉ Corso Ferrara 30 € varies 🚌 🚊 3, 9, 40, 62

Soundtown (5, B2)
This place is a cultural co-operative that offers a variety of artistic activities – from art to dance and plenty of jazz concerts, with performers from Piedmont and around the world. You can

also enjoy great cocktails and nibbles from 7pm every day, with a very suitable lounging soundtrack bubbling away in the background.
☎ 011 669 66 31
🖥 www.soundtown .it, Italian only ✉ Via Berthollet 25 🕙 11am-2am Mon-Fri, 6pm-2am Sat 🚌 to Piazza Madama Cristina

CLASSICAL MUSIC, OPERA, DANCE & THEATRE

RAI's symphony orchestra is based in Turin, and other excellent classical music companies perform on a regular basis. The opera season lasts from October to June, as does the classical ballet season. If you understand Italian you may want to catch a play – the theatre scene here is very lively.

Auditorium Giovanni Agnelli
In the Lingotto complex (6, A5), this is a wonderful place to hear the **Orchestra Sinfonica Nazionale della RAI** (www.orches trasinfonica.rai.it) in Renzo Piano–designed surrounds. Acoustics are fabulous.
☎ 011 664 04 58 🖥 www .expo2000.it ✉ Via Nizza 280 🚌 1, 35 🚊 18

Conservatorio Giuseppe Verdi (4, F6)
The home of the **Orchestra Filarmonica di Torino** (www.oft.it, Italian only) hosts a seasonal calendar of symphonic and chamber music.
☎ 011 436 06 91
🖥 www.conservatorio

-torino.it, Italian only ✉ Piazza Boldoni 🚌 🚊 to Porta Nuova

Teatro Alfieri (4, C3)
This old theatre on Piazza Solferino tends to show musicals and comedies that appeal to more mainstream tastes. Before booking, bear in mind that plays and performances will be in Italian.
☎ 011 562 38 00
🖥 www.torinospet tacoli.it, Italian only ✉ Piazza Solferino 4 🕙 box office 10am-10pm Mon-Sat, 2.30-10pm Sun 🚌 to Piazza Solferino

Teatro Carignano (4, F3)
Heartbreakingly beautiful, this is where Vittorio

Alfieri's *Cleopatra* was premiered in 1775. See also p36 for details on visiting the theatre.
☎ 011 517 62 46
🖥 www.teatrostabile .it ✉ Piazza Carignano 6 🚌 🚊 to Piazza Castello

Teatro Nuovo (5, C2)
With a lovely park location, this is a very good spot to see dance performances – especially if you're after modern and avant-garde styles. It also has a cinema on the premises.
☎ 011 650 02 11
🖥 www.teatronuovo torino.it, Italian only ✉ Corso Massimo d'Azeglio 17 🕙 box office 9am-7pm Mon-Sat, 3-7pm Sun 🚊 9, 16

Teatro Carignano, Piazza Carignano 6.

**Teatro Regio Torino
(4, G3)**
More an opera house than
a traditional theatre, the
Regio dates back to 1740.
However, little of the original interior remains after
a fire gutted the theatre
in 1936. Performances of
opera, ballet and classical
music are held here. For
smaller performances,
there's also the Teatro Regio
Piccolo in the complex.
☎ 011 881 52 41
🖳 www.teatroregio
.torino.it, Italian only
✉ Piazza Castello 215
🕙 box office 10.30am-
6pm Tue-Fri, 10.30am-
4pm Sat & 1hr before
performances 🚌 🚇 to
Piazza Castello 🦽 good

CINEMAS

The city is well served with cinemas, some of which screen films in their
original language. On average, expect to pay about €7 for a ticket. Bargain
day is Monday, with tickets generally reduced to €6. Foreign films are
generally dubbed (quite badly) into Italian, and sessions usually start at
about 3pm, with the last screening at around 10.30pm.

Lux (4, E4)
With a capacity of more
than 1000, Lux is worth a
visit for its fabulous
location, if nothing else,
inside Galleria San
Federico off Via Roma. Its
future often comes under
threat, but it seemed to be
hanging in there when we
visited.
☎ 011 54 12 83
✉ Galleria San Federico
🚌 🚇 to Piazza Castello

Massimo (4, H4)
Near the Mole Antonel-
liana, the Massimo offers
an eclectic mix of films,

mainly in English or with
subtitles. One of its three
screens is run by the Museo
Nazionale del Cinema (p8),
and screens only classic
films from its huge film
library.
☎ 011 812 56 58
✉ cnr Via Montebello
& Via Giuseppe Verdi
🚌 🚇 to Via Po

Pathé (6, B4)
This monster-sized multi-
plex in the Lingotto precinct
(6, B4) has 11 cinemas and
lots of mainstream and arty
Euro fare. Tickets here cost
€8, a tad pricey, but the

sound and image quality is
excellent.
☎ 011 667 78 56
✉ Lingotto, Via Nizza
230 🚌 1, 35 🚇 18
🦽 excellent 🚻

Romano (4, F3)
Located in lovely Gal-
leria Subalpina (4, F3), the
Romano plays arthouse
fare in its three smallish
cinemas. This a great spot
to catch Torino Film Festival
screenings.
☎ 011 562 01 45
✉ Galleria Subalpina
🚌 🚇 to Piazza
Castello

GAY & LESBIAN TURIN

Turin is not San Francisco, Berlin or Sydney, but it does have a gay scene of sorts and a few places to go out at night. For more information about places for cruising, you can visit Informagay's website at www.informa gay.it (Italian only).

Caffè Leri (4, C6)
The window display of a black mannequin sporting purple briefs invites you to enter this place, which is the pick of the bunch for many of Turin's night-owls, with a smart, stylish interior and a lively, friendly crowd of regulars who are fashionably dressed for the regular gay Saturday nights.
☎ 011 54 30 75 ✉ Corso Vittorio Emanuele II 64 ◷ 9pm-3am Tue-Sun 🚌 🚈 🚋 to Porta Nuova

Pink Strip
Juventus FC players originally wore a fetching shade of pink on the football field. It was only after a wrong shipment of shirts arrived from England, where they were manufactured in 1903, that the side made the switch to today's black-and-white striped strip.

Centralino (4, H5)
A mixed crowd frequents this straight club, but the youthful, populist vibe and great music is best enjoyed on one of its gay Sunday nights.
☎ 011 817 48 21 ✉ Via delle Rosine 16 € €10 ◷ midnight-5am Tue-Sun 🚌 🚋 to Piazza Vittorio Veneto

Il Male (3, E4)
Pubby and unpretentious, this low-key bar gets both gay and lesbian visitors and organises 'singles parties' with a straightforward meet-and-greet approach

to picking up (Thursday). Good snacks are also available.
☎ 011 28 46 17 ✉ Via Lombardore 10 ◷ 9pm-2am Tue-Sun 🚕 taxi

La Gare (3, C8)
Close to the train station (hence the name), this populist disco maintains mainstream musical tastes for a mixed gay and straight crowd. It's at its gayest on Saturday.
☎ 011 580 55 54 ✉ Via Sacchi 65 ◷ 11pm-6am Tue-Sat 🚌 🚈 🚋 to Porta Nuova

SPORT

Football

Turin's passion, like most other Italian cities, is for football *(calcio)*, and the city has one of the most famous (and, in recent times, successful) teams in Europe. **Juventus** (☎ 011 6 56 31; www.juventus.it), nicknamed 'La Vecchia Signora' (the Grand Old Lady) is top dog, with it's city rival **Torino** (www.toro.it,

Italian only) not as famous, but attracting devotion from local (and vocal) supporters. To see a match, purchase tickets (from around €20) from Ricordi Media Store (p64) or from tobacconists in the city. Games are generally played on Sunday. Unsold tickets for important games are rare as hen's teeth, but you may find something for smaller matches.

Stadio delle Alpi
This well known and imposing 67,000-seat stadium is located in the city's outer reaches, and comes complete with mountain views. Juventus are the big drawcard, but Torino play here as well.
☎ 011 73 29 47 ✉ Strada di Altessano 131 🚌 12, 62, 72, 75, 9b on match days 🚹 good

Sleeping

Turin is an Italian business hub, with plenty of conventions throughout the year and therefore many hotels geared towards business travellers. Most of these places tend to position themselves in the midrange to top-end blocks, with a dozen or so four-star piles keeping the bigwigs happy and one five-star hotel putting a roof over the heads of the jet set. Budget options do exist, although you'll find fewer of them than in other Italian cities.

Finding a bed needn't be a drama, especially at weekends, when many business travellers flee the city and most places reduce

Room Rates
These categories indicate the cost per night of a standard double room in high season.
Deluxe	from €201
Top End	€126-200
Midrange	€76-125
Budget	under €75

their rack rates – sometimes considerably. Arriving at a hotel in the middle of the week without a booking can sometimes be an act of faith – if there's a big convention on, you might find yourself out of luck. If you haven't booked a room yet for the Olympics, well…you're in for an interesting time.

Hotels are generally of a high standard in Turin, and while many three- and four-star joints subscribe to a 'grand but bland' design ethos, you'll find the service efficient and helpful and cleanliness a priority. Many hotels are located around Porta Nuova train station, a convenient spot

for transport and sightseeing. To enjoy the more edifying charms of the *centro storico* (historic centre), head for the streets that surround the central squares of Piazza San Carlo, Piazza Carlo Emanuele II and Piazza Castello. Prices are often higher, but you'll be within walking distance of the city's sights and its better restaurants. All of the following offer rooms with bathroom.

Accommodation booking can be arranged through any Turismo Torino tourist information office/ kiosk. See p112 for more details of contact information and locations. Feel free to ask any hotel for a discount or special deal – staff will often suggest them to you un-prompted if things are slow that week. For transport route information, see p114.

DELUXE

AB+ Living (4, E1)

Cooler-than-thou AB+ is a swanky interactive art–filled development in a beautiful medieval building near Porta Palatina and the duomo. It holds two penthouse suites and a 'tower house' plus plenty of luxury design details (Florence Knoll et al) and jet set bizkid facilities beloved by the types who keep very up to date with gadgets, fashion and whatever style rags tell them is hot right now. A buzzy bar is downstairs along with a wonderful restaurant, making this our number-one pick in Turin.
☎ 011 433 87 32
🖥 www.progettocluster .com ✉ Via della Basilica 13 🚌 🚋 to Porta Palazzo 🅿 ✖ AB+ (p72)

Grand Hotel Sitea (4, E5)

This haven of respectful, silky-smooth service plays host to the likes of the Juventus football team and visiting luminaries from the cinematic world when the film festival is on. Rooms are lavishly appointed, supremely comfy and solidly soundproofed – perfect for taking advantage of discounted weekend tariffs with someone you, er, like a lot.
☎ 011 517 01 71
🖥 www.thi.it ✉ Via Carlo Alberto 35
🚌 🚋 to Piazza Castello 🅿 ♿ ✖ Ristorante Carignano (p70) 🦽

Le Meridien Art + Tech (6, B4)

Cutting-edge design meets luxurious comfort at this fabulous annex of Le Meridien. It's a little bit slicker, a little bit sexier than its sister establishment in the Lingotto complex and perfect for business and pleasure. Floor-to-ceiling windows let the light flood in and the hotel's café seems to float in the city's fog. Mountain views, the best bathrooms in the city (with the best water pressure) and the coolest furnishings mean this is easily the city's most with-it place to rest your head.
☎ 011 664 20 00
🖥 www.lemeridien -lingotto.com ✉ Via Nizza 230 🚌 1, 35 🚋 18 🅿 ♿ ✖ Art + Café (p81)

Le Meridien Lingotto (6, A4)

This handsomely remodelled (thanks to Renzo Piano) building boasts sterling business facilities and silky-smooth service. If it's fitness facilities you're after, it's hard to go past the fact that you can treat the former FIAT test track on the roof as your jogging route. All rooms overlook the tropical garden in the centre of the building. If you're really out to impress, the *Scrigno* (jewellery box) suite, at a cool €3000 a night, will have you believing you're the reincarnation of Agnelli himself.
☎ 011 664 20 00
🖥 www.lemeridien -lingotto.com ✉ Via Nizza 262 🚌 1, 35 🚋 18 🅿 ✖ Torpedo (p81) ♿ 🦽

Star Hotel Majestic (4, D6)

Chances are, if you're staying here you're attending a conference or in town doing business, and the Star's business is making sure it all goes smoothly for you. Despite a busy location, rooms are incredibly quiet and the bar is a very nice place to escape a hard day's nodding in agreement. Considerable reductions are available for weekend stays.
☎ 011 53 91 53
🖥 www.starhotels .com ✉ Corso Vittorio Emanuele II 54
🚌 🚋 to Porta Nuova 🅿 ♿ 🦽

Soundproofing makes the Sitea *the* choice for work trips

TOP END

Albergo Genova e Stazione (5, A1)

The three-star Genova has recently had a thorough overhaul, and is a solid choice in this category. Part of the Best Western chain, service is by the book and facilities both well maintained and comfortable. Try to get a room on the top floor – they have that little bit more character and more generous proportions.

☎ 011 562 94 00
🖳 www.albergogenova
.it ✉ Via Sacchi 14b
🚌 🚈 🚇 to Porta
Nuova 🅿 ♿

Conte Biancamano (4, B6)

The Conte Biancamano boasts one of the loveliest sitting rooms we've seen, and some of the most helpful service we encountered in Turin. It's close to the train station of Porta Nuova and the central sights of the city, and while the bedrooms are not as fabulous as the communal areas, they are spotless and an obvious degree of care has been taken to avoid mundane uniformity. Excellent value in this price range.

☎ 011 562 32 81
🖳 www.hotelconte
biancamano.it ✉ Corso
Vittorio Emanuele II 73
🚌 🚈 🚇 to Porta
Nuova 🅿

Hotel Chelsea (4, E2)

Far removed from the notorious Chelsea Hotel in New York that tolerated the drug-addled behaviour of Bob Dylan, Brett Whiteley and Edie Sedgwick, this particular Chelsea is a family-run and family-friendly place with functional rooms and a flower-filled restaurant (with good prices for guests) that allows parents to dine while children sleep upstairs with a baby monitor. It's welcoming and so close to the action that you'll scarcely believe your luck if you score a weekend discount.

☎ 011 436 01 00
🖳 www.hotelchelsea.it
✉ Via XX Settembre 79
🚌 🚇 to Porta Palazzo
or Via XX Settembre
🅿 ♿

Hotel Concord (4, D6)

A four-star stalwart of the convention and conference circuit, the Concord exudes an individual charm by sporting well-worn Persian rugs in the lobby, a nicely stocked platter of lollies and a delightfully improvised pricing system that means if you just show up and they like the look of you, they'll come up with an offer you can't refuse. And the rooms? Tidy, tranquil and utterly impossible to differentiate from many other such establishments.

☎ 011 517 67 56
🖳 www.hotelconcord
.com ✉ Via Lagrange
47 🚌 🚈 🚇 to Porta
Nuova 🅿 ♿ ♿

Hotel Genio (5, B1)

Prominently announced by bright lights on porticoed Corso Vittorio Emanuele II, the Genio is part of the Best Western chain and operates on slick, efficient lines. Flower power seems to be the dominant decorative theme, with plenty of botanic motifs on the floors, beds and curtains, in a riot of fabric detail that aims for cosy and settles in at overload, mostly depending on how much coffee you've consumed that day.

☎ 011 650 57 71
🖳 www.hotelgenio
.it ✉ Corso Vittorio Emanuele II 47
🚌 🚈 🚇 to Porta
Nuova 🅿 ♿ ♿

Hotel Nazionale Torino (4, E5)

Fans of the horror flick *Profondo Rosso* will recognise this none-too-lovely example of Fascist-era skills with concrete. Inside, the décor is not staging any surprising lapses into relaxed good taste, but the rooms are serviceable and most have plenty of room to really strew your stuff around, plus the management's keen to haggle, so you can try for discounts of around 40% at weekends. The proximity to the glorious old cafés on Piazza San Carlo is another bonus.

☎ 011 561 12 80
🖳 www.hotelnazionale
.com ✉ Piazza CLN 254
🚌 🚈 🚇 to Porta
Nuova 🅿 ♿

Hotel Piemontese (5, B2)

You'll find this three-star charmer languishing in a 19th-century townhouse with a nice courtyard, and all trappings and trimmings are included, with the more

expensive rooms boasting spa baths and hydromassage implements. Plummeting weekend rates make it ideal for a semi-dirty escape (the bathrooms will generally render things cleaner than they should be).
☎ 011 669 81 01
🖳 www.hotelpiemontese.it ✉ Via Berthollet 21 🚌 🚊 🚉 to Porta Nuova or 🚌 to Piazza Madama Cristina 🅿 ♿ 🚶

Le Petit Hotel (4, D3)

Standing on the fringes of the *centro storico,* the friendly and helpful Petit has rather characterless 1980s rooms that nonetheless reflect the management's desire to keep things clean, tidy and well ordered. Rooms overlooking the internal courtyard tend to be quieter than those facing the street,

so make your preferences known early if you're a light sleeper. For visitors staying longer than a week, the newish rooms with kitchenette may appeal.
☎ 011 561 26 26
🖳 www.lepetithotel .it ✉ Via San Francesco d'Assisi 21 🚌 🚊 to Piazza Castello or 🚌 to Piazza Solferino 🅿 🚶

Residence Sacchi (3, C8)

Enter this old palace via a modern, bamboo-filled courtyard and stumble upon a colourful, modern range of apartments, suites and attics, all with excellent facilities for business travellers (all rooms have free Internet connections). In a very handy location, the opportunity to really spread out and treat the place as you own home makes it particularly good value in this price range. Excellent

discounts apply for weekly or monthly bookings too.
☎ 011 556 38 11
🖳 www.residence sacchi.it ✉ Via Sacchi 34 🚌 🚊 🚉 to Porta Nuova 🅿

Turin Palace Hotel (5, A1)

Turin's last word in late-19th-century luxury, the Turin Palace combines tastefully decorated rooms with very convenient proximity to the train station. Modern gadgetry is effortlessly incorporated into all 122 rooms, making it an excellent business choice, and reductions of around 30% apply at weekends.
☎ 011 562 55 11
🖳 www.thi.it ✉ Via Sacchi 8 🚌 🚊 🚉 to Porta Nuova 🅿 ♿

Victoria Hotel (4, F5)

The Victoria has established such a 'home away

The Turin Palace Hotel flies the flag for modern good taste

from home' reputation that it's often fully booked. It boasts marble-clad walls, reassuringly stuffed floral sofas, wood panelling galore and a British sensibility that makes everyone feel they're in a safe place.

Renovations were being done when we visited, meaning that there should be some additional rooms on offer by the time you read this, although with any luck, the intimate atmosphere will be retained.

Some rooms have gorgeous mountain views.
☎ 011 561 19 09
🖥 www.hotelvictoria
-torino.com ✉ Via Nino Costo 4 🚌 🚊 to Piazza Castello or Porta Nuova
🅿 ♿

MIDRANGE

Hotel Amadeus (4, H5)
The Amadeus is a quiet, efficiently run three-star hotel that offers some rooms with kitchenette facilities, making this handy for self-caterers. It's close to Via Po, Piazza Vittorio Veneto and the Mole Antonelliana, plus Turin's university, meaning that eating and nightlife are close for those who have no intention of self-catering. Ask for a discount, you'll probably get one.
☎ 011 817 49 51
🖥 www.turinhotelcom pany.com ✉ Via Principe Amedeo 41bis 🚌 🚊 to Piazza Vittorio Veneto

Hotel Bologna (4, C6)
The lobby promises little, but in a reversal of many Italian two-star hotels, the rooms at the Bologna are better than you'd guess. The management's friendly, the location excellent and many rooms have been updated in recent times, which means that penny pinchers (it's a whisper from being a budget hotel) have long been clued-up about this place, so you'd do well to reserve a room well in advance.
☎ 011 562 01 91
🖥 www.hotelbologna rsrl.it, Italian only ✉ Corso

Vittorio Emanuele II 60
🚌 🚊 🚊 to Porta Nuova
🅿 ♿

Hotel Boston (3, C8)
Room rates at this funky, arty La Crocetta hotel can swing between midrange and top end, and the décor swings between minimalist chic and ethnic knick-knackery, but you'll probably want to spend most of your time in the communal areas, scoping the owner's exciting art collection that features works by famous modern

artists such as Andy Warhol, Piero Ruggeri and Lucebert. Service is helpful, and the attached restaurant highly recommended.
☎ 011 50 03 59
🖥 www.hotelboston torino.it ✉ Via Massena 70 🚊 4, 16 🅿 ✖ Casa Vicina (p79) ♿

Hotel des Artistes (4, G4)
No, you won't exactly be enveloped in a Moulin Rouge–style environment here, but you will experience secure, professional

See the staircase of Liberty at the Hotel Dock & Milano

A 'classical' Quadrilatero Romano hotel; the Hotel Dogana Vecchia

hotel living in a handy neighbourhood. It's reassuring with no surprises (good or bad) up its sleeve, and rooms are bright, clean and soundproofed. Single rooms are available for €89, but fork out an extra €10 or so and you can have a double all to yourself.

☎ 011 812 44 16
🖥 www.desartisteshotel
.it ✉ Via Principe Amedeo
21 🚌 🚊 to Via Po Ⓟ

Hotel Dock & Milano (3, B6)

Worth it for making an entrance and an exit via the grand Liberty staircase alone. You'll find rooms here spacious and elegant, with plenty of character supplied by wooden floors, natural light and attractive furniture. Located near Porta Susa train station, which is due to become Turin's main train hub, this place can only get more popular with time,

so it might be wise to book ahead.

☎ 011 562 26 22
🖥 www.dockmilano
.com ✉ Via Cernaia 46
🚌 🚊 🚊 to Porta Susa
or Piazza Statuto 🍴 🚴

Hotel Dogana Vecchia (4, D2)

The charming Dogana Vecchia, a 17th-century inn, has boasted Mozart and Verdi among its guests and offers a warm welcome in the Quadrilatero Romano. Modern rooms lack the simple elegance of the older rooms, so see if you can snaffle one of the older versions, although basic amenities are found in both. It's within easy walking distance of the *centro storico*'s sights, and some of the city's best eating and drinking options. The internal parking is a selling point in itself.

☎ 011 436 67 52
🖥 www.hoteldogana

vecchia.com ✉ Via Corte d'Appello 4 🚌 🚊 to Porta Palazzo or Piazza Castello Ⓟ

Hotel Liberty (4, E3)

The lovely old Liberty is aptly named, as it's situated in an area known for this style of early 20th-century architecture. It's well managed and genteel, priding itself on attracting 'noble ladies, artists and people of culture and business'. Not to mention Lonely Planet readers, who often recommend this place due to its charm and some of the positively enormous rooms available.

☎ 011 562 88 01
🖥 www.hotelliberty
-torino.it ✉ Via Pietro
Micca 15 🚌 🚊 to Piazza
Castello Ⓟ 🚴

Hotel Roma e Rocca Cavour (4, D6)

Literary types will be interested to note that

writer Cesare Pavese is said to have spent his last days at this historic hotel before committing suicide in 1950. Others will simply be interested to know that this great hotel has all the trappings for an atmospheric stay, from creaky parquet floors to a few Liberty-style trappings and a 'we'll get round to it' approach to redecorating. You're close to both Porta Nuova train station

and the shopping on Via Roma. There are also triple rooms available, and good weekend discounts.

☎ 011 561 27 72
🖳 www.romarocca.it
✉ Piazza Carlo Felice 60
🚌 🚊 🚃 to Porta Nuova

Hotel Solferino & Artuá (4, C4)
The old wooden-and-glass elevator that takes you to this delightful establishment sometimes gives the impres-

sion that it won't make it. Relax, it does, and once ensconced in this grandiose old townhouse you might find it hard to leave. The phrase 'old-fashioned charm' seems perfect for such a place, and the service is textbook in terms of courtesy.

☎ 011 517 53 01
🖳 www.hotelartua.it
✉ Via Brofferio 1
🚌 to Piazza Solferino
or 🚌 🚊 🚃 to Porta Nuova 🅿 🏃

BUDGET

Ai Savoia (4, C1)
Located in an 18th-century townhouse near one of the *piazze* in the city's most interesting quarter, Ai Savoia offers three classically styled rooms, two of which retain their original wood-beamed ceilings. The gilt-laden breakfast room overlooks Piazza Savoia and should get your day started in style. All rooms sleep at least two people, and the management's accommodating and friendly. A jewel.

☎ 339 125 77 11
🖳 www.infinito.it/utenti/aisavoia ✉ Via del Carmine 1b 🚌 52, 60 🅿

Albergo San Giors (3, D5)
The modest but welcoming San Giors is within spitting distance (quite literally) of the Porta Palazzo market and a lively immigrant area. It's a clean, friendly option with triple rooms also available, a cosy eatery on the premises, and breakfast included in the prices.

☎ 011 521 12 56
🖳 sangiors@energy

united.it ✉ Via Borgo Dora 3 🚌 🚊 to Porta Palazzo 🍴 San Giors (p75)

B&B Aprile (3, C5)
This charming establishment offers three small, distinctive apartments on the top floor of a 16th-century building in the city's most atmospheric quarter. The crumbling flight of steps is an adventure in itself, but the real fun begins when you explore this delightful 'hood, with gorgeous Piazza della Consolata right behind you and the Porta Palazzo markets convenient for self-caterers. Cristina, the owner, is a friendly, extremely helpful delight. All apartments have been renovated using natural materials and a lot of skill from Cristina's partner, Ugo.

☎ 011 436 01 14
🖳 www.aprile.to.it
✉ Via delle Orfane 19
🚌 🚊 to Porta Palazzo

B&B Casamarga (4, J5)
This relaxed B&B exudes a *'mia casa e tua casa'* informality and is a couple

of skips from Piazza Vittorio Veneto, and therefore some of the city's best summer nightlife. There is only one split-level bedroom for use (it sleeps up to three), and there's a large kitchen where breakfast is served. Pets, and their owners, are welcome.

☎ 011 88 38 92, 339 437 10 86 🖳 casamarga@hotmail.com ✉ Via Bava 1bis 🚌 🚊 to Piazza Vittorio Veneto 🏃

Hotel Nizza (5, A1)
The Nizza is a good safe bet in an area not known for its obvious charms. Recently restored, it has nice-sized rooms, which, while not exactly oozing individuality, are bright, comfortable and orderly. Ignore the extortionate breakfast and source your own in the city centre. A little English is spoken – it gets better if you steer the conversation onto rugby.

☎ 011 669 05 16
🖳 hotelnizza@infinito.it ✉ Via Nizza 9
🚌 🚊 🚃 to Porta Nuova 🏃

About Turin

HISTORY
Hannibal

During the Second Punic War (218–202 BC), Piedmont's mountains proved the mightiest enemy. Carthaginian general Hannibal crossed the Italian Alps and en route stumbled across Taurasia (Turin) on the River Po, home to the Taurini tribe since between 500 and 400 BC. Hannibal burnt the village to the ground.

Caesar

Julius Caesar founded Colonia Giulia (Turin) in 58 BC, granting Roman citizenship to its inhabitants. During the 40-year rule of Roman Emperor Augustus (from 43 BC), the Roman *castrum* (fort) was refounded as Augusta Taurinorum and fortified with 6m-high walls, pierced by four gates. The eastern city gate (incorporated into the façade of Palazzo Madama; p20) and its northern counterpart (Porta Palatina; p35) still stand.

The Savoys

The immensely influential Savoy dynasty had gained a foothold in Piedmont as early as 1046 with the marriage of Adelaide, heiress of Turin County, to Oddone of Savoy (1010–60). In 1248 the Savoys scored complete control of Turin and – with the exception of a brief interlude between 1255 and 1274 (when rebellious Turinese sided with the Republic of Asti to oust the Savoys) – ruled the Piedmontese capital almost exclusively until the 19th century.

In 1347 the bubonic plague tore through Europe, killing off half of Turin's population and leaving economic depression and famine in its wake. The Black Death, as the disease was otherwise known, didn't thwart Savoy growth.

Palazzo Carignano, birthplace of Victor Emanuele II

Dos & Don'ts
- In rainy weather, umbrellas are allowed no further than the threshold. Most shops, cafés, restaurants and museums sport a soggy-brolly stand at their entrance.
- Dress modestly in churches – no shorts, short skirts or bare shoulders. Avoid visiting a church during Mass or other services.
- Shopping in Turin requires etiquette; killer glares from shop assistants will establish if you're doing things right or wrong. Stroking and fondling is frowned upon – ask if you want to try on a garment or inspect it more closely.
- Don't expect an orderly queue anywhere. Things such as the order of service seem to be done on intuition and the system seems to work. Sometimes.
- Don't assume anyone cares whether you're subjected to second-hand cigarette smoke or mind-numbing, second-hand mobile telephone conversations.

In 1536, the French seized Piedmont, maintaining control of it throughout the Italian Wars (1494–1559). Duke of Savoy Emanuele Filiberto (1553–80) shifted the Savoy capital from Chambéry in present-day France to Turin in 1563, and set about building elegant palaces and public buildings. The duke's glorification of the city was continued by Carlo Emanuele I (1580–1630), Vittorio Amedeo II (1666–1732) and Carlo Emanuele II (1638–75).

Turin was besieged by French and Spanish troops in 1706, inciting its population to seek refuge in the citadel (p30) and prompting Pietro Micca to blow up a tunnel – and himself – to stave off French advances.

Napoleon & Cavour

The concept of national sovereignty grew with the arrival of Napoleon Bonaparte and his troops, who marched into Turin and forced the Savoys into exile in 1798. Turin-born Camillo Benso di Cavour (1810–61) fought side by side with Giuseppe Garibaldi to break the stranglehold of foreign domination with his brilliant diplomacy. The palace in Turin where Cavour was born and died can be visited (p27).

After the resignation of Piedmont prime minister Massimo d'Azeglio, Cavour took his place and focused on forging an alliance with the French emperor Napoleon III, in a move destined to overthrow Austrian domination of Piedmont.

The Kingdom of Italy was declared on 17 March 1861. Vittorio Emmanuel II became the first king of Italy, and Turin became the kingdom's capital, a status it kept until 1865, when the parliament and capital shifted to Florence.

FIAT & Fascism

In 1899, the Fabbrica Italiana di Automobili di Torino (FIAT) was founded. Fascism's rise after WWI was paralleled by that of trade unionism. Industrial unrest on the factory floors of FIAT spawned the Italian

Tiny and well-kept Fiat parked somewhere in Turin

Communist Party in 1921 under the leadership of Antonio Gramsci (1891–1937), a Turin university graduate.

During WWII, allied bombings destroyed vast areas of Turin. The city was liberated from the Germans and Italian fascists in May 1945, after Allied troops broke through German lines.

Turin Today

In January 2003, when FIAT boss Giovanni Agnelli succumbed to prostate cancer, aged 83, it seemed to outsiders that the very soul of Turin had died with him. Hot on the heels of his death, the firm, which his grandfather founded, announced job cuts worldwide and the closure of 12 factories, in a last-ditch attempt to save a company that had seen two straight years of billion-euro losses. However, Turin is not the sort of city that dwells in its past, and is currently undergoing one of the world's largest-ever urban rejuvenation programmes. It is directing its considerable energy and nous towards the technical-scientific sectors (rather than traditional manufacturing) and is enjoying an artistic renaissance that has seen it emerge as the centre of contemporary art in modern Italy.

ENVIRONMENT

The Po – Italy's longest river at 652km – traverses the entire Piedmont region, flowing east from its Alpine source at the foot of Monviso. Other notable rivers include the Dora Baltea, Sangone and Stura di Lanzo – all of which meet the Po at Turin.

Air pollution menaces Turin: carbon monoxide emissions create a filthy headache thanks to the city's over-zealous motorists (Italy ranks third in the world after the USA and Australia for the number of cars per capita). In 1999 a token handful of electric cars and buses were introduced in Turin, followed every year since by a series of car-free days in the city centre. A newish project called carcityclub (www.carcityclub.it,

Italian only) aims to encourage car-pooling, thus reducing carbon monoxide emissions.

That said, Turin is a savvy place that has made a concerted effort to shake off its industrial image, with urban recycling programmes, successful preservation initiatives and constant reminders thanks to alpine views that the environment is one of the most important issues on the city's agenda – especially if the city wants a big green tick for the 2006 Winter Olympics.

GOVERNMENT & POLITICS

Turin is the capital of the Piedmont region and of the Provincia di Torino (Turin Province). Left-wing Sergio Chiamparino, whose party landed a third term in office in 2001, is the city's mayor. Elections to Piedmont's *consiglio regionale* (regional assembly) in January 2005 ushered in Lega Nord (Northern League) party member Oreste Rossi as president. The youthful Allesandria-born politician's election demonstrates a degree of sympathy with the Lega Nord's push for more genuine autonomy from the central government.

ECONOMY

In 2006 Turin will host the Winter Olympics. This means big bucks. Not counting investments from within Piedmont, €2.6 billion in Olympic and government funds is being ploughed into the area. Supposedly, for every €1 million spent, 15 new jobs will be created – peaking at 9700 by 2005. New state-of-the-art sporting venues and hotels are being built at competition venues in Turin, the Valle di Susa and Val Chisone; and transport infrastructure is being radically improved. Unemployment will fall by 0.3% a year and annual GDP will rise by 0.3% to 0.4% – an increase in value of €1.4 billion between 2004 and 2007 – according to Toroc (Torino Organising Committee), the brain behind the Olympic extravaganza. That said, funding shortfalls were already causing headaches and hand-wringing in 2004, and as is often the case with Olympic events, the final balance sheet may read differently to the PR balance sheet.

Did You Know?
- Population: 897,000
- Elevation: 239m
- Parkland: 17 sq metre per person
- Mobile phone users: About 60% of people aged 11 or over
- Unemployment rate: 6%
- Average number of children per woman: 1.13

SOCIETY & CULTURE

Locals are accustomed to hard work and working hard. They are resilient and resourceful, with a steely determination and independence spawned by their city's industrial heritage. Caginess toward and suspicion of anyone not from Turin is a result of the mass immigration of workers from southern Italy to the regional capital in the 1960s. The entrepreneurial energy

And the band plays! Here at the central Piazza San Carlo

and creativity that many Turinese possess was also kindled by industry, which prompted people to dream up new means of making money.

Optimism with a good sense of humour, passionate loyalty to friends, and a passion for wine, food, football and cars, are classic labels worn across the region and especially in Turin. *Piemontese falso e cortese* (literally 'false and kind', meaning appearing to be generous but actually the contrary) is a common expression, although you'll generally find that people are, quite simply, polite and not as tight with money as you may have heard. A head for business is admired though – so if you're here for that you'll want to look the part and act smart. Anyone familiar with the barrage of personal questions that usually goes hand in hand with meeting people in the *mezzogiorno* (southern Italy) may be pleasantly surprised to find themselves left in relative peace in Turin.

Strolling beneath the porticoes of Turin's Via Roma on Sunday is an eye-opener. First come the well-dressed and well-heeled, out to buy cake for traditional family Sunday lunch. Next come the Juve fans, en route to the football stadium for the Sunday match. Then there's the afternoon horde, a younger crowd that hails from suburbia and hits the centre to hang out. Tradition, as in most of Italy, plays an important role in local life, but you'll also find that Turin looks to its future more noticeably than other Italian cities. Traditional dynamics have shifted and with a new wave of migration and economic change – there's a shift that's putting a focus more and more on new technologies and cultural growth, and on seeing that Turin receives the recognition and admiration it deserves.

Putting a Label On It

Label – essential reading for any contemporary arts, architecture, fashion, style and culture fiend – is *ID*, *Wallpaper* and *DazedAndConfused* rolled into one. The Turin-based avant-garde mag (www.labelmag .com) is published quarterly.

ARTS
Architecture

Baroque Turin will dominate your architectural tour of the city, and with good reason. As royal architect to the Savoys from 1615, Carlo di Castellamonte (1560–1641) worked on Castello del Valentino (p32), among others. The city was further enlarged under Guarino Guarini (1624–83), who specialised in chapels and churches. Under Filippo Juvarra (1678–1736), the Savoy capital became an architectural masterpiece: look no further than Palazzina di Caccia di Stupinigi (built 1729; p21) or Basilica di Superga (built 1715–31; p15) to see why.

In the 19th century Alessandro Antonelli (1798–1888), from eastern Piedmont, conjured up the most fabulous silhouette on Turin's skyline, the Mole Antonelliana (p8).

Wonderful examples of 20th-century *Stilo Liberty* (Art Nouveau) can be found throughout the city, especially along Corso Francia (3, B5), and in the posh bastions of La Crocetta and La Collina. Giacomo Mattè Trucco (1869–1934) original FIAT factory in Lingotto (built 1926) – a five-storey concrete monster that Le Corbusier hailed as a 'cathedral of technology' – was an industrial marvel.

Rationalist architect Pier Luigi Nervi (1891–1979) designed the Palavela (built 1961), with its innovative sail-shaped roof. At the time of writing it was undergoing a refurbishment at the hands of noted architects Gae Aulenti and Arnaldo de Bernardi.

Turin leads the way in Italian contemporary architecture, thanks partly to its role as 2006 Winter Olympic host (p28). The University of Turin's new Humanities faculty, on the industrial banks of the Dora,

Basilica di Superga

was designed by Norman Foster, while Massimiliano Fuksas provided the creative inspiration behind the futuristic glass-towered Palazzo della Regione (built 2001–04) and the new building that will grace the Porta Palazzo markets (p12). Turin is also an excellent city for the repurposing and rejuvenation of former industrial sites such as Docks Dora and Lingotto, which, in 1988, saw Italian architect Renzo Piano start transforming the factory into a hi-tech cultural-centre-cum-shopping-mall, complete with conference room in a blue glass bubble and an art gallery (p16) in a steel 'treasure box'.

Literature

Modern Italian literature was ushered in by Edmondo de Amicis (1846–1908) with his novel, *Cuore* (1886), the tale of a boy's schooldays in Turin. Palermo-born Natalia Ginzburg (1916–91) spent most of her life in Turin, evoking her adopted city in semi-autobiographical novels such as *Tutti i Nostri Ieri* (All Our Yesterdays; 1952).

Giulio Einaudi (1912–99) opened his publishing house in 1931. The intellectual published dozens of politically inspired books after WWII, including the Communist works written in prison by Antonio Gramsci.

Fascism nurtured a wealth of novelists, including Cesare Pavese (1908–50), who spent his literary career in Turin; his greatest novel, *La Luna e Il Falò* (The Moon and the Bonfire; 1950) was published the year he committed suicide in his room at Hotel Roma e Rocca Cavour (p101).

Like Pavese, Turinese doctor Carlo Levi (1902–75) experienced internal exile in southern Italy under fascism. The result was *Cristo si è Fermato ad Eboli* (Christ Stopped at Eboli; 1945), a moving account of an oppressed world forgotten by Rome.

Liberia Biggio

Cinematic Turin

Turin has been used as a backdrop for scores of films, not just *The Italian Job*. Check out the following flicks if you can: horror-movie maker Dario Argento's *Profondo Rosso* (Deep Red; 1975) and *Non Ho Sonno* (Sleepless; 2001); *La Donna della Domenica* (The Sunday Woman; 1976) by Luigi Comencini (in which someone is bizarrely bludgeoned to death by a ceramic phallus); Mimmo Calopresti's *La Seconda Volta* (The Second Time; 1995); and *Così Ridevano* (1998), directed by Gianni Amelio. The multicultural face of modern Turin is painted in *Tango Story* (2003), a film about an Argentinian immigrant tangoing around the city.

Turin-born Jew Primo Levi (1919–87) ended up in Auschwitz. His poetry collection, *Se Quest è Un Uomo* (If This is a Man; 1958), is the dignified account of his survival. *Other People's Trades* (1985) includes an account of the Turin apartment at Corso Re Umberto 75, where he committed suicide (by throwing himself down a stairwell in the apartment block).

Music

Mau Mau (www.maumau.it, in Italian) and Subsonica steal the show in Turin's dynamic contemporary-music scene. The Mau Mau trio generates an eclectic sound with its innovative use of language (a mix of Italian, French, Spanish and Piedmontese dialect) and acoustics.

Turinese production house PiemonteGroove (www.piemontegroove.com) works with electronic dance artists, including funk DJ Roger Rama; experimental DJ Lorenzo LSP; the Nig Nig Nig duo; and Eiffel 65, a three-man band known for its mix of pop, techno and acid house. The band's DJ element, Turin-born Gabry Ponte (www.gabryponte.com, in Italian), topped the Italian club charts with his first solo single in 2001.

DJs Sergio Ricciardone and Giorgio Valletta are the faces behind Xplosiva (www.xplosiva.com, Italian only), a Turin-based project that fuses funk with break beat, house and techno.

Named after Turin's No 77 bus route, which took them to rehearsals, Linea 77 (www.linea77.com) is a five-piece rock band with a clutch of albums – *Too Much Happiness Makes Kids Paranoid* (2000), *Ketchup Suicide* (2001) and *Numb* (2003) – to its name.

If you're after something a little more laid-back, then Turin-born Carla Bruni's French-language debut album *Quelqu'Un M'a Dit* is every bit the smooth fare you'd expect from the city's fave supermodel-turned-chanteuse.

Drummer at concert at Piazza Vittorio Veneto

Directory

La Stampa, all the news printed to fit since 1867

ARRIVAL & DEPARTURE

Air

Turin airport (TRN; 1, B2; ☎ 011 567 63 61; www.aeroportoditorino .it) is located 16km northwest of the city centre in Caselle. International destinations include London, Barcelona, Frankfurt, Munich, Brussels, Lisbon, Madrid and Paris; national flights serve Rome, Naples, Palermo, Bari, Cagliari, Catania and Pescara. Turin is also linked directly by bus to Milan's international **Malpensa Airport** (MXP; ☎ 02 7485 22 00; www.malpensa .com, Italian only), 100km to the northeast.

INFORMATION

Airport Tourist Office   ☎ 011 567 81 24;
   🕑 8.30am-10pm

Car Park	☎ 011 567 63 61/2
Flight Information	☎ 011 567 63 61/2
Lost Property	☎ 011 567 62 00
Ticket Office	☎ 011 567 63 73

AIRPORT ACCESS
Bus

Sadem (☎ 011 300 01 66; www .sadem.it, Italian only) runs buses to the airport from Stazione Porta Nuova (40 minutes), stopping also at Stazione Porta Susa (30 minutes). Buses depart every 30 minutes between 5.15am and 10.30pm (6.30am and 11.30pm from the airport).

Single tickets (€5) are sold at Porta Nuova at **Caffè Cervino** (4, C6; Corso Vittorio Emanuele II 57). Buses stop on the corner of Corso Vittorio Emanuele II and Via Sacchi (4, C6). At Stazione Porta Susa, **Bar Milleluci** (3, B6; Piazza XVIII Dicembre 5) sells tickets.

At the airport, you can buy tickets at the tourist office in the arrivals (domestic/EU flights) hall, from the automatic ticket machine inside the main entrance, at the tobacconist in the arrivals area

or, for an extra €0.50, on the bus. Buses arrive and depart from the stop in front of the arrivals hall (domestic flights exit).

Taxi

A taxi between the airport and the centre of town will generally cost between €30 and €36 and takes approximately 30 minutes. Call ☎ 011 57 37 or ☎ 011 57 30 if there are none at the arrivals area.

Train

From Stazione Dora, trains leave for the airport every 30 minutes between 5.13am and 7.43pm. Tickets for the 20-minute journey cost €3.

Bus

Most national and international buses terminate at and depart from Turin's **bus station** (3, B7; ☎ 011 433 25 25; Corso Castelfidardo; 🕑 ticket office 6.30am-1.25pm & 2-8.30pm Mon-Sat, 6.30am-1.15pm & 2-8.30pm Sun; international ticket office 9am-12.30pm & 3-7pm Mon-Fri, 9am-12.30pm Sat).

For the UK and Continental Europe, **Eurolines** (☎ 055 35 71 10; www.eurolines.it) links Turin with a number of European cities including London, Paris, Barcelona and Prague.

Car & Motorcycle

Turin lies at the centre of Piedmont's extensive road network, and is also a major staging post on the overland route to France. The major motorways serving Turin are the A4, which traverses the north of Italy passing by Milan on the way to Venice; the A5 for Ivrea and Aosta; the A6 for Savona and the Ligurian coast; the A21 for Asti and Alessandria; and the A32 for the Valle di Susa ski resorts and the Fréjus tunnel into France.

Train

Turin is an important rail junction, with regular departures for major cities including Rome, Milan and Venice. International trains currently run to Paris, Lyon and Barcelona. The city's two main train stations are Stazione Porta Nuova (4, D4) and Stazione Porta Susa (3, B6). At the time of research, major work was under way to make Porta Susa the city's main train station, in time for the 2006 Winter Olympics.

Travel Documents
PASSPORT

As a rule a valid passport is all you need to enter the country.

VISA

Italy is a signatory of the Schengen Convention, so there are no checks at borders with other Schengen countries (all EU member countries except the UK, Ireland, Iceland, Norway and the newest 10 countries). Legal residents of one Schengen country do not need a visa for another. UK and Irish nationals are also exempt from visa requirements for Schengen countries. Nationals of Australia, Canada, Israel, Japan, New Zealand, Switzerland and the USA do not require visas for tourist stays of up to 90 days to any Schengen country. South African nationals require visas for Italy.

Customs & Duty Free

There is no limit on the amount of euros brought into Italy. Goods brought in and exported within the EU incur no additional taxes, provided duty has been paid somewhere within the EU and the goods are for personal consumption.

Duty-free sales within the EU no longer exist. Visitors coming from non-EU countries can import, duty-free, 1L of spirits, 2L wine, 60mL perfume, 250mL eau de toilette, 200 cigarettes and other goods to a total of €175.50; anything over this must be declared and the duty paid. On leaving the EU, non-EU citizens can reclaim any Value Added Tax (VAT) on purchases over €155 from shops that display a 'tax-free for tourists' sign.

Left Luggage

You can store luggage at **Stazione Porta Nuova** (☎ 011 669 04 45; 🕒 6am-midnight) for €3.50 for the first five hours, then €0.30 per additional hour.

GETTING AROUND

Throughout this guide we've listed the most obvious bus, tram and train options for getting to attractions, restaurants, hotels and the like by naming the most obvious street, piazza or stop from which to alight. You'll often find though, that Turin is just as easy to explore on foot, as it's flat and distances are generally short. Keep in mind that by the time you read this, the metro system may be a better option for travelling between certain sights. Turin and its environs are served by **GTT** (☎ 800 99 00 97; www.gtt.to.it), which publishes a large, confusing fold-out map of its transport routes (available at tourist information points). The city boasts a dense network of buses, trams and a cable car. GTT has an **information office** (🕒 7am-9pm) at Stazione Porta Nuova.

Buses and trams run from about 5am to midnight and tickets cost €0.90 for 70 minutes unlimited travel (€1.80 for four hours between 9am and 8pm and €3 for a one-day pass). Tickets are sold at tobacconists, the automatic ticket dispensers at train stations, and larger bus and tram stops. To validate your ticket, punch it in the orange machines on board buses, trams and the cable car.

Useful Transport Routes

The following bus/tram routes are suited for the following areas. Please note that due to extensive public works these routes may change:

Lingotto	🚃 18	🚌 1, 35
Piazza Castello, Via Po and Piazza Vittorio Veneto	🚃 13, 15	🚌 55, 56
Piazza Solferino		🚌 5, 14, 29, 59
Piazza Statuto and Porta Susa	🚃 13	🚌 1, 10, 29, 36, 51, 56, 59, 65
Porta Nuova	🚃 4, 15	🚌 11, 12, 33-35, 61, 63, 64
Porta Palazzo	🚃 3, 4, 16	🚌 11, 12, 19, 50
Via Cernaia	🚃 13	🚌 29, 55, 72
Via Lagrange	🚃 18	🚌 61, 68
Via and Piazza Madame Cristina	🚃 18	🚌 67
Via XX Settembre and Via Milano	🚃 4	🚌 11, 12, 27, 50, 51, 57
Vittorio Veneto	🚃 13, 15	🚌 55, 56

Travel Passes

The Torino Card (p117) gets you free public transport for the duration of the card's time limit. If you're in town for a while, buy an *abbonamento mensile*, which has unlimited travel for a calendar month on the urban transport system (€32).

Bus

Buses are either orange or grey and blue, and clearly marked, as are route numbers and destinations. Each stop has a large sign showing what routes use that stop and the stops made by each service, with an arrow indicating direction.

Tram

Service numbers 3, 4, 10, 13, 15, 16 and 18 are all trams. Each tram stop will have a large sign showing what routes use that stop and the stops made by each service, with an arrow indicating direction.

Metro

In 2006 the first section of Turin's brand new metro is set to open. Line 1 of the €975 million project will connect Collegno in the west with Stazione Porta Nuova, while a second line is to run from Stazione Porta Nuova to Lingotto Fiere. The 8.4km of Line 1 will be accessed by 15 stations, with a further six being constructed for the shorter 3.9km second line. For more information, refer to www.metrotorino.it.

Train

The vast majority of trains (at the time of writing) terminate at **Stazione Porta Nuova** (4, D6; Piazza Carlo Felice). Turin's other train stations are **Stazione Porta Susa** (3, B6; Corso Inghilterra), **Lingotto** (6, A2; Via Panunzio 1) and **Stazione Dora** (3, C3; Piazza Baldissera).

Bicycle

Cycling is a popular pastime in Turin. Before pedalling off, ask at a tourist office for the excellent *Carta dei percorsi ciclabili di Torino* (1:17,500, free), which maps all of the city's 40km of cycle paths. Alternatively go to www.comune.torino.it/ambiente/bici/percorsi.html to view the routes.

Parco Valentino Cycles (3, D9; Viale Ceppi, Parco del Valentino; per hour/day/weekend €2/8/11; ☺ 3-7pm Mon-Fri, 10am-1pm & 3-7pm Sat & Sun Mar, Apr & Oct, 3-10pm Mon-Fri, 9am-10pm Sat & Sun May-Sep) has bikes for a park-wide pedal, take bus 9 or tram 16. **Parco della Colletta Cycles** (Via Carcano, Parco della Colletta; per hour/day/weekend €2/8/11; ☺ 3-7pm Mon-Fri, 10am-1pm & 3-7pm Sat & Sun Mar, Apr & Oct, 3-10pm Mon-Fri, 9am-10pm Sat & Sun May-Sep), located northeast of the Cimtero Generale (General Cemetery), is a popular destination for families and is on the River Dora.

Taxi

Hailing a cab, as in whistling and waving your arm, doesn't work in Turin. Telephone for one or wait at a taxi rank. Reliable operators include **Centrale Radio** (☎ 011 57 37) and **Radio Taxi** (☎ 011 57 30). **GTT** (☎ 011 818 32) operates a service for disabled people.

If you phone for a taxi, the driver will turn on the meter immediately and you'll pay the cost of travel from wherever the driver receives the call. Taxis are metered, so always make sure the meter is switched on.

Car & Motorcycle

On a short trip to Turin, you're unlikely to need your own wheels, and the traffic congestion, parking restrictions and environmental impact will not make driving here a pleasant experience.

There are 24-hour petrol stations on the corner of Corso Vittorio Emanuele II and Corso Massimo d'Azeglio (5, C2); and on Piazza Borromini (3, F7).

ROAD RULES

Despite what you've seen and heard, Italy's road rules follow international norms. Drive on the right and overtake on the left; wear seat belts; turn headlights on outside built-up areas; carry a warning triangle; and don't drink and drive. The blood-alcohol limit is 0.05%.

Speed limits, unless otherwise indicated by local signs, are: 130km/h on *autostrade*; 110km/h on main roads; 90km/h on secondary roads; and 50km/h in built-up areas.

Driving is limited in parts of the *centro storico* (historic centre). The area between Piazza Statuto and Piazza Castello, comprising Via Garibaldi and several nearby streets, is closed to traffic.

RENTAL

Turin is compact and public transport is efficient and inexpensive.

If you do need to hire a vehicle you could try the following:
Avis (☎ 011 50 11 07; www.avis.com; Stazione Porto Nuova)
Europcar (☎ 011 650 36 03; www.europcar.com; Stazione Porta Nuova)
Maggiore (☎ 011 661 46 29; www.maggiore.it; Stazione Porta Nuova)

DRIVING LICENCE

All EU member states' driving licences are fully recognised throughout Europe. If you have a non-EU licence you'll need an International Driving Permit, available from your national automobile association. It's valid for 12 months and must be kept with your regular licence. Costs vary from country to country, but count on about €10.

PARKING

Finding a park on city streets is a nightmare. Thankfully, the Turinese don't care who parks where, meaning it's acceptable to abandon your vehicle in the middle of certain streets (literally) or on the pavement for a short time. Street parking (in the official blue spaces) costs from €0.50 to €2 per hour. Tickets are available from meters, tobacconists and newsagents.

To leave your car in an authorised car park costs from €0.40 to €1.30 per hour.

The following are the city's major car parks:
Parcheggio Emanuele Filiberto (3, D5; Piazza Emanuele Filiberto) 100m from Piazza della Repubblica, 110 spaces
Parcheggio Lingotto (6, B4; Via Nizza 294) 4000 spaces
Parcheggio Madama Cristina (5, B2; Piazza Madama Cristina) 259 spaces, and 2hr free with Torino Card
Parcheggio Roma (4, D6; Piazza Carlo Felice) In front of Stazione Porta Nuova, 348 spaces and 2hr free with Torino Card
Parcheggio Valdo Fusi (4, F5; Btwn Via Giovanni Giolitti, Via San Francesco da Paola, Via Camillo Cavour & Via Accademi Albertina) 480 spaces

PRACTICALITIES
Business Hours

Shops open from 9am or 10am to around 1pm and 3.30pm to 7.30pm (or 4pm to 8pm) Monday to Saturday; many are closed on Monday morning. In Turin, larger shops and department stores open Sunday afternoon and until 10pm some evenings. Many supermarkets operate 'nonstop', meaning 9am to 7.30pm Monday to Saturday.

Opening hours of museums and galleries vary; many close on Monday. Banks open from 8.30am to 1.30pm and 3.30pm to 4.30pm weekdays. Post offices open from 8.30am to 5pm or 6pm Monday to Friday and 8.30am to 1pm on Saturday. Pharmacies open from 9am to 12.30pm and 3.30pm to 7.30pm Monday to Friday and Saturday mornings. A couple in Turin run a night service.

Bars and cafés open from 7.30am to 8pm. Clubs and discos open around 10pm; in Turin the scene stays busy until around 3am, and often 6am on weekends.

Many businesses and shops close for part of August.

Climate & When to Go

Summers are always hot and humid in Turin, and winters, while cold, are quite tolerable although the fog can be thick as soup. The best time of year to visit is generally Spring or Autumn, although those into Winter sports will find the best skiing from December to March. The heaviest rainfalls occur in April, May and June.

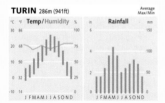

TURIN 286m (941ft)

For a weather forecast, follow the *'meteo'* link on the Regione Piemonte website (www.regione.piemonte.it). For ski resort weather reports, see www.torino2006.org.

Consulates & Embassies

Most countries have an embassy or consulate in Turin or Milan as well as in Rome.

Australia (☎ 02 77 70 41; australian-consulate-general@austrade.gov.au; 3rd floor, Via Borgogna 2, Milan, 20122)
Canada (☎ 02 6 75 81; Via Vittorio Pisani 19, Milan, 20124)
France (4, D5; ☎ 011 573 23 11, 011 561 95 29; Via Roma 366, Turin, 10123)
Germany (4, A5; ☎ 011 53 10 88; Corso Vittorio Emanuele II 98, Turin, 10121)
UK (3, C8; ☎ 011 650 92 02; www.britain.it; Via Saluzzo 60, Turin, 10125)
USA (☎ 02 29 03 51; www.usembassy.it; Largo Donegani 1, Milan)

Disabled Travellers

Turin, like many Italian cities, is getting its infrastructure ready for travellers with impaired mobility, with many of the city's attractions revamping facilities for the 2006 Winter Olympics. We've included icons in our listings to assist travellers with their choices of sights, restaurants and hotels. Listings in this book that are wheelchair-friendly are marked by the ♿ icon and rated 'limited', 'good' and 'excellent'. 'Limited' denotes a minimal level of accessibility, 'good' reflects a partial level of access, while 'excellent' applies to places that offer full access to sights and attractions.

Public transport in Turin is improving – with one third of the city's buses, half of all trams and (soon) the metro system able to transport wheelchairs *(carrozzelle)*. When you call a cab (☎ 011 581 16), let the operator know that you want to transport your wheelchair.

Many galleries and museums in the city (as well as ATMs) provide hearing loops, plus modern buildings and recently restored buildings will generally have textured floors for vision-impaired visitors.

INFORMATION & ORGANISATIONS

Piedmont offers disabled travellers help through Turin-based **Informa Handicap** (4, E2; ☎ 011 442 16 31; informahandicap@comune.torino .it; Via Palazzo di Città 11; ☿ 9am-noon & 1.30-4pm Mon-Fri). Online, **Consulta Persone in Difficoltà** (☎ 011 319 81 45; www.comune .torino.it/itidisab, in Italian) publishes sightseeing itineraries.

Discounts

The **Torino Card** (48/72 hours for €15/17) includes free admission into 120 museums and monuments in Piedmont, and 50% discount on selected theatre and concert tickets, bicycle hire, guided visits and so on. In Turin, card-holders travel for free on public transport, get a 50% discount on suburban transport and a free ride on a River Po boat, the Sassi-Superga tram and the Mole Antonelliana's panoramic lift. In Turin the tourist office and some hotels sell the card.

STUDENT & YOUTH CARDS

An International Student Identity Card (ISIC) and a Euro<26 card provide discounts. **Centro Turistico Studentesco e Giovanile** (4, H4; CTS; ☎ 011 812 45 34; www .cts.it; Via Montebello 2h) in Turin sells both cards.

Electricity

Voltage	220V
Frequency	50Hz
Cycle	AC
Plugs	Two or three round pins

Emergencies

Turin is not a dangerous city – you're unlikely to come across vio-lence – but care should be taken to avoid pickpockets who, as in all major Italian cities, are active. Bag snatching is not a common occurrence, but it pays to wear the strap of your bag or camera across your body and facing the side away from the road. There is a police station *(questura)* located at Corso Vinzaglio 10 (3, B6; ☎ 011 5 58 81).

The streets east and south of Stazione Porta Nuova have an unpleasant reputation according to some, although in recent times the area has undergone something of a transformation and is quite popular as a night-time destination.

Parked cars, particularly those with foreign number plates or rental-company stickers, are prime targets for thieves. Never leave valuables in your car.

Ambulance	☎ 118
Fire	☎ 115
Police	☎ 112

Fitness

For details about cycling, see p115, and for golf, see p43. For winter sports such as skiing, see Out & About (p50).

GYM

Try **Palestra Il Pardo** (4, F6; ☎ 011 88 39 00; www.ilpardo.it; Via Accademia Albertina 31; ☿ 9am-10.30pm Mon-Fri, 9am-6pm Sat, 9.30am-1.30pm Sun), which has arrangements with hotels in the city, enabling you to visit and use its fine facilities.

JOGGING

Turin's love affair with its own cooking means that you'll never be lonely if you want to jog around the city. Popular areas for a run include **Parco del Valentino** (3, D8) and **Parco della Colletta**.

SWIMMING

There's a covered swimming pool at **Centro Nuoto Torino** (☎ 011

35 54 73; Corso Sebastopoli 260; €3.79/3.24; 🕑 12.30-3pm Mon-Fri, 9.30am-6pm Sat), although under 16s can only swim there between 2.30pm and 3.30pm on Saturday.

Gay & Lesbian Travellers
Turin has an active gay and lesbian scene that dates from the early 1970s and a nightlife that's inclusive and extroverted. Despite general acceptance, you may not always feel comfortable with public displays of affection in certain parts of town.

INFORMATION & ORGANISATIONS
It was from the organisation Fuori! that **Informagay** (6, A2; ☎ 011 85 17 43; www.informagay.it, Italian only; Via Giordano Bruno 80) sprang, though **Matisse** (4, E2; ☎ 011 562 34 14; Via Giuseppe Garibaldi 13) is viewed as the birthplace of Turin's gay movement.

Both Informagay and **Circolo Maurice** (4, E1; ☎ 011 521 11 16; www.mauriceglbt.org/php/index .php, Italian only; Via della Basilica 3) can direct you to gay entertainment spots, or go online at www .gay.it/guida/Piemonte

Health
IMMUNISATION
No jabs are required for a trip to Italy. The water is safe to drink.

MEDICAL SERVICES
In Italy, medical care is freely available to EU nationals carrying an E111 form, but citizens of non-EU countries should make sure they have arranged appropriate insurance. Everyone (including foreigners) can receive treatment in a casualty ward *(pronto soccorso)*, or in any public hospital, where you can also get emergency dental treatment.

Ospedale Mauriziano Umberto I (3, B9; ☎ 011 5 08 01; Largo Turati 62) accepts emergency patients.

PHARMACIES
Pharmacies stock most medicines and are able to advise on general medical matters. A list is posted at every pharmacy advising the nearest after-hours pharmacy. There is a **pharmacy** (4, D6; ☎ 011 518 64 67; Stazione Porta Nuova; 🕑 7am-7.30pm) located inside Stazione Porta Nuova.

Holidays
Most Italians take their annual holiday in August. *Settimana Santa* (Easter Week) is another busy holiday period for Italians. Following are national public holidays:
New Year's Day 1 January
Epiphany 6 January
Good Friday March/April
Easter Monday March/April
Liberation Day 25 April
Labour Day 1 May
Republic Day 2 June
Patron Saint's Day (San Giovanni) 24 June
Feast of the Assumption 15 August
All Saints' Day 1 November
Feast of the Immaculate Conception 8 December
Christmas Day 25 December
Feast of Santo Stefano 26 December

Internet
INTERNET SERVICE PROVIDERS
If you are taking your notebook or palmtop computer with you, take a universal AC adaptor and a European plug adaptor. For more information, see www.teleadapt.com.

AOL (www.aol.com) and **CompuServe** (www.compuserve.com) have dial-in nodes in Italy (☎ 702 000 50 32).

INTERNET CAFÉS
1PC4YOU (4, H4; ☎ 011 83 59 08; Via Giuseppe Verdi 20g; per hr €2-6; 🕑 9am-9pm Mon-Sat, 2-8pm Sun) Hourly rates vary depending on the number of people surfing.
FNAC (4, E3; ☎ 011 551 67 11; Via Roma 56; per 30min/hr €2/3; 🕑 9.30am-

8pm Mon-Sat, 10am-8pm Sun) Only four terminals, but a very central location.

USEFUL WEBSITES
City Vox www.cityvox.com; general listings guide
Comune di Torino www.comune .torino.it/canaleturismo/en/index.html; practical information from the city authority
Extra Torino www.extratorino.it; comprehensive, up-to-date listings guide in English
Lonely Planet www.lonelyplanet .com; for reliable travel advice about Italy and the rest of the world
Torino 2006 www.torino2006.org; Olympic facts and figures
Turismo Torino www.turismotorino .com; extensive tourist information in English

Lost Property
Airport (☎ 011 567 62 00) Baggage claim area ⏱ 8am-midnight
GTT (☎ 011 442 92 46) For items lost on the city's public transport network

Metric System
The metric system is standard and, like other continental Europeans, Italians use commas in decimals and points to indicate thousands.

TEMPERATURE
°C = (°F - 32) ÷ 1.8
°F = (°C x 1.8) + 32

°C		°F
50		120
	45	110
40		100
	35	90
30		80
	25	70
20		
	15	60
10		50
	5	40
0		30
	-5	
-10		20
	-15	10
-20		0
	-25	-10
-30		-20
	-35	-30
-40		-40

DISTANCE
1in = 2.54cm
1cm = 0.39in
1m = 3.3ft = 1.1yd
1ft = 0.3m
1km = 0.62 miles
1 mile = 1.6km

WEIGHT
1kg = 2.2lb
1lb = 0.45kg
1g = 0.04oz
1oz = 28g

VOLUME
1L = 0.26 US gallons
1 US gallon = 3.8L
1L = 0.22 imperial gallons
1 imperial gallon = 4.55L

Money
ATMS
ATMs are abundant in Turin, and multilingual.

CHANGING MONEY
You can change money in banks, at the post office or in a *cambio* (exchange office). Out of hours, try a 24-hour banknote-exchange machine – Turin has a couple.

CREDIT CARDS
Visa, MasterCard and other major credit cards are widely accepted – except at some toll booths on the motorway and in many budget hotels, pizzerias and smaller *trattorie*, which only accept cash.

If your credit card is lost, stolen or taken by an ATM, cancel the card immediately on these numbers:
American Express ☎ 06 722 82
MasterCard ☎ 800 870 866
Visa ☎ 800 877 232

CURRENCY
The euro is the official currency; one euro is divided into 100 cents. Coin denominations are one, two, five, 10, 20 and 50 cents, €1 and €2. Notes are €5, €10, €20, €50, €100, €200 and €500.

TRAVELLERS CHEQUES
To cash travellers cheques, you need your passport as ID. If you lose your travellers cheques call:
American Express ☎ 800 872 000
Thomas Cook/
 MasterCard ☎ 800 872 050
Visa ☎ 800 874 155

Newspapers & Magazines
For local and regional news, try *La Stampa* (www.lastampa-nordovest .it, in Italian), a 50-page broadsheet going since 1867. Entertainment listings are included in *Torino Sette*, the Friday insert of *La Stampa*; cinema, theatre and exhibition listings are included in its

daily *Spettacoli Cronaca* section. If the latest in contemporary art and culture excites you, the publication *cluster* (www.progettocluster .com), from the same people who run AB+ (see p72), is a bilingual delight.

Photography & Video

Taking photos or filming inside churches and museums is frowned upon and you may find yourself receiving a lecture if you ignore the signs telling you not to do so.

Post

Francobolli (stamps) are sold at post offices and tobacconists. Italy's postal service doesn't have a great reputation, but most things seem to get there eventually. Count on up to two weeks for letters to the UK or USA, and two to three weeks to reach Australia. For more information visit www.poste.it.

Post restante can be sent to Ferma Posta, at the **Central Post Office** (4, D4; ☎ 011 506 02 92; Via Alfieri 10; 🕑 8.30am-7pm Mon-Fri, 8.30am-1pm Sat), with the receiver's name, and the post office address.

POSTAL RATES

To send a letter weighing up to 20g by *posta ordinaria* (regular airmail) costs €0.41 within Europe and €0.52 to other destinations.

Posta prioritaria (priority mail) guarantees delivery within Europe (€0.62 for a letter up to 20g) in three days and the rest of the world (€0.77) in four to eight days. For urgent mail, use *postacelere*, the post office's courier service. Important or valuable items are best sent by *posta raccomandata* (registered mail; €2.58/2.94 for up to 20/100g) or *posta assicurata* (insured mail), the cost of which depends on the value of the item being sent (10% of the object's value, within Europe).

Radio

For news events and chat, take your pick from Radio Torino Populare (97 FM) or Radio Piemonte Stereo (90.7 FM). For contemporary music, check out Radio Veronica One (93.6 FM) or, for a more electronic sound, Radio Energy (93.9 FM). For music and gossip with a student slant, listen to Radio Blackout 2000 (97 FM).

Telephone

To call Italy from abroad, dial the country code (☎ 39) and the telephone number (*including* the initial zero). For mobile phones, drop the zero. *Numeri verdi* (toll-free numbers) start with ☎ 800, and the prefixes ☎ 848 or ☎ 199 indicate calls charged at a local rate.

To make an international call from Italy, dial ☎ 00, country code, city code and telephone number.

PHONECARDS

Telecom Italia (www.telecomitalia .it) has a liberal sprinkling of orange public payphones in the streets and train stations of Turin. Phones accept Telecom Italia phonecards (valued at €5, €10 and €20), sold at post offices, tobacconists, newsagents, and in vending machines at train stations. There's a **Telecom Italia centre** (4, E3; Via Roma 18; 🕑 8am-10pm) with public pay phones.

A local/national call from a public phone costs €0.10/0.20 for three to six minutes, depending on the time of day.

MOBILE PHONES

Italy uses GSM 900/1800 (compatible with the rest of Europe and Australia, but not North American GSM 1900 or the system in Japan). Mobile-phone numbers start with a four-digit prefix, such as 0330, 0335 or 0347. Drop the initial zero when calling from abroad.

TIM (Telecom Italia Mobile; www.tim.it, Italian only) and **Vodaphone** (www.vodafone.it, Italian only) offer *prepagato* (prepaid) accounts for GSM phones, from as little as €10. **Wind** (www.wind.it) is the only dual-band operator.

COUNTRY & CITY CODES
Italy has no area codes; the 'code' (eg ☎ 011 for Turin) is an integral part of the telephone number and must always be dialled.

Italy	☎ 39
Turin	☎ 011

USEFUL PHONE NUMBERS
Although there are no guarantees, you can expect the operator to have reasonably basic English for things like collect calls and international inquiries.

Directory enquiries	☎ 12
International directory enquiries	☎ 176
Operator-assisted calls (collect calls) to Europe	☎ 15
Operator-assisted calls (collect calls) to elsewhere	☎ 170
Info 412 (cinemas, pharmacies, weather & traffic reports)	☎ 142

Television
Italy's commercial stations are Canale 5, Italia 1, Rete 4 and La 7, as well as state-run RAI 1, RAI 2 and RAI 3 (programme listings for all three at www.rai.it, in Italian). The Italian TV industry started in Turin about 50 years ago, but that doesn't mean you'll escape the diet of mind-numbing variety shows, histrionic talk shows and more cleavage than seems necessary for even this breast-obsessed country.

Time
Turin is one hour ahead of GMT. Daylight-saving time, when clocks are moved forward one hour, starts on the last Sunday in March. Clocks are put back an hour on the last Sunday in October. Italy operates on a 24-hour clock.

Tipping
Tipping is not an entrenched practice in Italy, and service is often included in the bill at a restaurant. Rounding up the bill to the nearest euro is always appreciated though.

Toilets
Public toilets? You'll no doubt end up popping into a bar or a café instead. Some places may frown if you don't buy a coffee first, but most establishments are used to this, and locals do it too.

Tourist Information
Atrium Torino (4, C4; ☎ 011 53 59 01/011 53 51 81; www.turismotorino .com; Piazza Solferino; ⏰ 9.30am-7pm Mon-Sat, 9.30am-3pm Sun)
Informacittà (4, D2; ☎ 011 442 28 88; Piazza Palazzo di Città 9a; ⏰ 8.30am-6pm Mon-Fri, 9am-1pm Sat) City information service
Stazione Porta Nuova (4, D6; ☎ 011 53 13 27; ⏰ 9.30am-7pm Mon-Sat, 9.30am-3pm Sun) A branch of the City Tourist Office

Women Travellers
Turin is an easy destination for women travellers, although solo women will probably draw the attention of a bewildering array of Italian men and feel at risk of hearing *'Ciao Bella'* ad infinitum. Shake off an unwanted Romeo by ignoring him, telling him you have a *marito* (husband) or *fidanzato* (boyfriend), or simply walking away.

LANGUAGE
Many locals speak at least some English, exposed as they are to the constant influx of foreign business travellers. Still, any attempt to speak Italian will be appreciated. Here are some useful phrases to get

you started. Grab a copy of Lonely Planet's *Italian phrasebook* if you'd like to know more.

Basics

Hello.	*Buongiorno.* (pol)
	Ciao. (inf)
Goodbye.	*Arrivederci.* (pol)
	Ciao. (inf)
Yes.	*Sì.*
No.	*No.*
Please.	*Per favore/*
	Per piacere.
Thank you.	*Grazie.*
You're welcome.	*Prego.*
Excuse me.	*Mi scusi.*
Sorry	
(forgive me).	*Mi perdoni.*
Do you speak English?	*Parla inglese?*
I don't understand.	*Non capisco.*
How much is it?	*Quanto costa?*

Getting Around

When does the...	*A che ora*
leave/arrive?	*parte/arriva... ?*
bus	*l'autobus*
boat	*la barca*
train	*il treno*
I'd like a... ticket.	*Vorrei un biglietto di...*
one-way	*solo andata*
return	*andata e ritorno*
Where is... ?	*Dov'è... ?*
Go straight ahead.	*Si va sempre diritto.*
Turn left/right.	*Giri a sinistra/destra.*

Accommodation

a hotel	*un albergo*
Do you have any rooms available?	*Avete delle camere libere?*
a... room	*una camera...*
single	*singola*
twin	*doppia*
double	*matrimoniale*
a room with bathroom	*una camera con bagno*

Around Town

I'm looking for...	*Cerco...*
the market	*il mercato*
a public toilet	*un gabinetto*
the tourist office	*l'ufficio di turismo*
What time does it open/close?	*A che ora (si) apre/chiude?*

Eating

breakfast	*prima colazione*
lunch	*pranzo*
dinner	*cena*
The bill, please.	*Il conto, per favore.*

Shopping

How much is it?	*Quanto costa?*
Do you accept... ?	*Accettate... ?*
credit cards	*carte di credito*
travellers cheques	*assegni per viaggiatori*

Time, Days & Numbers

What time is it?	*Che ora è?*
today	*oggi*
tomorrow	*domani*
yesterday	*ieri*
morning	*mattina*
afternoon	*pomeriggio*
day	*giorno*
Monday	*lunedì*
Tuesday	*martedì*
Wednesday	*mercoledì*
Thursday	*giovedì*
Friday	*venerdì*
Saturday	*sabato*
Sunday	*domenica*
1	*uno*
2	*due*
3	*tre*
4	*quattro*
5	*cinque*
6	*sei*
7	*sette*
8	*otto*
9	*nove*
10	*dieci*
100	*cento*
1000	*mille*

Index

See also separate indexes for Eating (p125), Sleeping (p126), Shopping (p126) and Sights with map references (p127).

EATING

SLEEPING

SHOPPING

Sights Index

FEATURES

La Pista	*Eating*
Da Giancarlo	*Entertainment*
Dual	*Drinking*
Al Bicerin	*Café*
Mole Antonelliana	*Highlights*
Shoeco	*Shopping*
Carlina	*Sights/Activities*
AB+ Living	*Sleeping*

AREAS

Beach, Desert
Building
Land
Mall
Other Area
Park/Cemetary
Sports
Urban

HYDROGRAPHY

River, Creek
Intermittent River
Canal
Swamp
Water

BOUNDARIES

State, Provincial
International
Ancient Wall

ROUTES

Tollway
Freeway
Primary Road
Secondary Road
Tertiary Road
Lane
Under Construction
One-Way Street
Unsealed Road
Mall/Steps
Tunnel
Walking Path
Walking Trail
Track
Walking Tour

TRANSPORT

Airport, Airfield
Bus Route
Cycling, Bicycle Path
Ferry
General Transport
Metro
Monorail
Rail
Taxi Rank
Tram

SYMBOLS

Bank, ATM
Buddhist
Castle, fortress
Christian
Diving, Snorkeling
Embassy, Consulate
Hospital, Clinic
Information
Internet Access
Islamic
Jewish
Lookout
Monument
Mountain
National Park
Parking Area
Petrol Station
Picnic Area
Point of Interest
Police Station
Post Office
Ruin
Swimming Pool
Telephone
Toilets
Zoo, Bird Sanctuary
Waterfall

24/7 travel advice

www.lonelyplanet.com